THE DOCTRINE & COVENANTS

KEY TO SHARING THE GOSPEL *with* PLAINNESS & SIMPLICITY

RANDY L. BOTT

CFI
An imprint of Cedar Fort, Inc.
Springville, Utah

ISBN 13: 978-1-4621-3790-9

Published by CFI, an imprint of Cedar Fort, Inc.
2373 W. 700 S., Springville, UT 84663
Distributed by Cedar Fort, Inc., www.cedarfort.com

Library of Congress Control Number: 2020948524

Cover design by Shawnda T. Craig

Edited and typeset by Valene Wood

Printed in the United States of America

10 9 8 7 6 5 4 3 2 1

Printed on acid-free paper

To my ever-faithful wife, Vickie, who lives what she teaches.

To the thousands of missionaries and students, who learned and grew with me as we discovered how to more effectively share the gospel.

To Leaun Otten, who kindled in me a love of the Doctrine and Covenants.

Contents

Introduction

This Book Is Written for You

Whether you are a young man or a young woman preparing to serve a full-time mission, a young person who hasn't yet decided to serve, a married couple preparing children to serve, or a senior couple wondering if a mission is right for you—this book is for you.

However, each of the above descriptors merely states the station where you are on your journey through life. That is not who you really are. In order to put you into eternal perspective you need to understand and accept that you are a literal spirit son or daughter of Heavenly Parents.

Your birth on earth was preceded by a very lengthy maturing period in the presence of our Heavenly Parents. You had already distinguished yourself as one of the "noble and great ones" (see Abraham 3:22) by choices you made in that pre-earth life.

You were decidedly on the Lord's side during the war in heaven. You were "ordained" to "minister to the inhabitants of the world in the Grand Council of Heaven before this world was" (see *Teachings of the Prophet Joseph Smith*, 365). "Ordinations" are only preformed after calls have been issued and accepted by those called. So, our calls to minister to the inhabitants of the earth were given, accepted, and empowered by the Lord before we were ever born.

You were designated by the Savior as "the salt of the earth" realizing that very little salt (compared to the entire loaf) was necessary but absolutely essential to season the entire loaf (see Matthew 5:13).

You are not here on earth at this time by accident. God knew exactly when you would be born, how long you would live, and how far you would travel (see Acts 17:26). In fact, God determined the entire population of this earth according to His chosen people—the Children of Israel (see Deuteronomy 32:8–9).

You were held in reserve for 6000 years for this very time to fight the battles with Satan and his armies for the souls of men during the final time before the Millennium. Satan knows you well and all of us, to one degree or another, can testify to the truth that Joseph Smith and Sidney Rigdon saw in a vision: "Wherefore, he [Satan] maketh war with the saints of God, and encompasseth them round about" (D&C 76:29).

However, you were not sent to earth to fail. All have stumbled and fallen but thanks to the Atonement of Christ, we are able to get up, repent, and rejoin the battle.

"There has been a day of calling, but the time has come for a day of choosing; and let those be chosen that are worthy" (D&C 105:35). That verse refers directly to you!

That is who you really are: chosen, ordained, preserved. "For ye are lawful heirs, according to the flesh, and have been hid from the world with Christ in God" (D&C 86:9).

Now is your hour—something you have waited for. Something you "shouted for joy" for (see Job 38:7). Something the Lord has foreordained and prepared you for—for over 6,000 years. Don't make the mistake of turning away from this signal honor. You are literally one in millions to be so honored to serve with the Lord as the Millennium fast approaches.

Being called and chosen comes with the responsibility to be prepared. Just putting on a black name tag isn't sufficient. Just showing up at the MTC with your suitcases but with little preparation would be like showing up at the starting line of a marathon race without any prior training.

Now is the time to get serious, no matter what your present station is in life. Now is the time to "come join the ranks" and prove to yourself and the Lord that you are worthy to inherit the kingdom He has prepared for the faithful.

Background for writing this book

I am writing this book looking back on 39 years of professional teaching, with a three-year interlude while my wife and I served as mission president. The last nineteen years I have spent teaching Missionary Prep and Doctrine and Covenants at BYU–Provo. According to their records, I taught over 55,000 students during those nineteen years.

Because there was not a formal curriculum for the Missionary Preparation course when I started teaching, I was asked to create my own course outline. My directions were: Teach them what you wished they had known before coming to you in the mission field. Teach them how to cope with the challenges your missionaries faced that diminishes their effectiveness. And teach them the Atonement of Jesus Christ, the Plan of Salvation, and the doctrines of the Restoration.

With that direction and mandate, I started to teach. Each semester I found myself adjusting my course outline—adding to what I had been teaching and dropping some of the topics of lesser importance. At the same time, I was teaching mostly Missionary Prep, I was also teaching the scriptural "love of my life"—the Doctrine and Covenants.

As time progressed, I realized that I was teaching more and more from the Doctrine and Covenants in my Missionary Prep classes. However, it wasn't until I retired and had time to reflect over my teaching career that I discovered that I may have spent more unnecessary time and energy creating my own curriculum for Missionary Prep when the Lord had already revealed it to Joseph Smith and the early Brethren.

Before it was published and released to the Church, along with many others, I had the privilege of working on the draft copy of *Preach My Gospel.* In no way is this meant to suggest it was anything other than what was said of it: "A document designed in heaven and written on earth." In writing this book, I am certainly not suggesting this is better than *Preach My Gospel*—it is just another approach to better prepare missionaries (young and old) to share the gospel.

Preach My Gospel is used in every MTC as a training manual. It is also used in the mission field for continued polishing and perfecting the missionaries. This book is designed to better prepare future missionaries so when they arrive at the MTC they are ready to hit the road running.

In this book I will focus on several issues at once: the problems, the solutions, the doctrines, and the sequence. In revealing what is now numbered as Section 1, the Lord commanded: "Search these commandments, for they are true and faithful, and the prophecies and promises which are in them shall all be fulfilled" (D&C 1:37).

From my experience as a mission president and also serving for four years in a branch presidency at the Provo MTC, it was a rare treat to find a missionary who had read the entire Doctrine and Covenants. Virtually none of the missionaries could list more than a limited number of prophecies or promises the Lord had made in the Doctrine and Covenants.

No one will argue that the Lord is the Master Teacher and Role Model for us to follow. Then why not let Him model the details of missionary preparation as He moved Joseph Smith and the early Brethren from spiritual infancy through the various steps towards exaltation?

The sequential approach will demonstrate doctrine and principles as the Lord molded and shaped His future leaders and brought faithful investigators to an understanding of the gospel. Some of the doctrine will be consolidated in order to avoid redundancy.

The ancient apostle Paul, probably one of the greatest and most successful missionaries of all time, taught his "son in the faith" Timothy, a principle that will be employed throughout this book:

> Thou therefore, my son, be strong in the grace that is in Christ Jesus. And the things that thou hast heard of me among many witnesses, the same commit thou to faithful men, who shall be able to teach others also. Thou therefore endure hardness, as a good soldier of Jesus Christ. No man that warreth entangleth himself with the affairs of this life; that he may please him who hath chosen him to be a soldier. And if a man also strive for masteries, yet is he not crowned, except he strive lawfully. *The husbandman*

> *that laboureth must be first partaker of the fruits.* Consider what I say; and the Lord give thee understanding in all things. (2 Timothy 2:1–7, emphasis added)

For emphasis, consider these points contained in those verses:

1. Teach what you have been taught so others can continue to teach thus causing a "snowball" effect carrying your influence far beyond those you can personally teach.
2. You will have very little power or influence unless you connect with that endless power supply—Jesus Christ.
3. Leave all your worldly cares behind when you go on your mission. Focus on sharing the gospel. Then you will be acceptable to the Savior and empowered by Him.
4. The next point (italicized above) is very important and will provide the format for the book: *First you must experience the gospel yourself before you can, with power, teach it to others.* For example, how can you teach people to get an answer to prayer if you have never recognized an answer yourself? How can you teach people to repent and receive forgiveness of their sins if you have never repented and experienced the soul-thrilling effects of being forgiven?

How the book is constructed:

The first part of every chapter will help you better understand the doctrine and how to apply in your own life the principles the Lord teaches His early missionaries in this dispensation. The second part of the chapter will run parallel to the first part but will give some limited suggestions on how to teach the principle to investigators and Church members whose understanding needs to be increased. It will also contain some cautions and areas to avoid.

From years of personal missionary experience, I will try to identify some obstacles you may face as you teach the restored gospel to others.

I will not be able to identify all barriers, but I can forewarn you about some challenging questions which may be asked (both sincere questions and those intended to entrap you).

Although the principles and doctrine will come from the Doctrine and Covenants, all four standard works will be tied together to arm you with the necessary understanding to face and overcome the satanic opposition which will undoubtedly come as you become an effective instrument in the Lord's hands to spread His gospel to the world.

How to use the book:

You can read straight through the book or go to the chapters you are most interested in. Take time to look up the scriptural references that I refer you to but are not written out in the book.

Ideally you would study with your parents or other adult mentor. They will have insights and ideas that are not contained in the book. Some of the doctrine is very deep and will require adult discussion for you to understand. You might also study the different topics with your friends who are also preparing for missions.

If you want to get the most from your study, try teaching what you are learning to your family—at Family Home Evening, or to your friends. In a perfect world, you could try teaching the doctrine to friends who are not yet members of the Church. Any experience you get in learning to express yourself on religious topics will give you a great head start when you begin your mission.

If you don't understand some of the scriptures or doctrine in the book, ask questions. The more experience you have in answering difficult or challenging questions about the gospel, the more comfortable you will be when you are confronted in the mission field.

Don't expect to understand or remember everything you read in this book the first time through. Review often the doctrine and scriptures so they become familiar to you. Your mission will be like a two-year or eighteen-month marathon. You wouldn't expect to just show up the day of the race without training and expect to win the race. Prepare now for an exciting and life-changing marathon that you have been foreordained to before the world was created.

Jesus Christ

The Author, Atoner, and Power

There are two sections of this book which do not fit into a numbered chapter format. This is one of them and the overview of the plan of salvation is the other. Why the exception for this section? Because Jesus Christ is the umbrella under which everything else happens. Without His Atonement, without His creative power, without His championing the Father's plan, we would not exist. As King Benjamin noted: "I say unto you that if ye should serve him who has created you from the beginning, and is preserving you from day to day, by lending you breath, that ye may live and move and do according to your own will, and even supporting you from one moment to another—I say, if ye should serve him with all your whole souls yet ye would be unprofitable servants" (Mosiah 2:21).

Therefore, every principle, doctrine, and practice written in this book, and the hundreds of priceless gems which are not included, all have a lifeline connecting them back to the Savior. It will take you a lifetime and longer to fully know the Father and the Son. But succeeding in your quest will result in your gaining eternal life. "And this is life eternal, that they might know thee the only true God, and Jesus Christ, whom thou hast sent" (John 17:3).

In one glorious burst of light, God shattered forever the false notion that the heavens were sealed. The First Vision will be discussed in Chapter 1. However, the contents of this section will reveal the cause for some of the hatred and vicious attacks that you will likely endure as you magnify your calling as a missionary and as you spread the good news of the restoration.

After a brief introduction by God, the Father, Jesus Christ became the voice orchestrating the restoration. In answer to Joseph Smith's inquiry about which church to join, Joseph records the following: "I was answered that I must join none of them, for they were all wrong; and the Personage who addressed me said that *all their creeds were an abomination in his sight; that those professors were all corrupt;* that: 'they draw near to me with their lips, but their hearts are far from me, they teach for doctrines the commandments of men, having a form of godliness, but they deny the power thereof'" (JS—History 1:19, emphasis added).

Nothing could strike nearer the heart of today's Christianity than the very Person central to all Christianity saying, "all of their [foundational] creeds were an abomination." The professors being corrupt didn't necessarily mean they were bad people. They were corrupt in the sense that they were mixing the philosophies of men with scripture thus making it nearly impossible for people to discover the pure, uncorrupted truth leading them back to the presence of God. They also denied the need for priesthood, the necessity of saving and exalting ordinances, and the visions and revelations God desires to bestow upon His children.

As your interest grows, you may want to search online for "Nicene Creed," "Trinity," and other words and phrases which will greatly expand your understanding why the Savior would say those creeds were an abomination.

As you study the Savior's life and ministry and as you become more familiar with His person, you will likely ask: "How was He able to do what He did?" Although we have much to learn (most of which will probably happen in the next life), He gives a partial answer in Doctrine and Covenants 93:2–5 (emphasis added):

> And that I am the true light that lighteth every man that cometh into the world;
>
> And that I am in the Father, and the Father in me, and the Father and I are one—

> The Father because *he gave me of his fulness*, and the Son because I was in the world and made flesh my tabernacle, and dwelt among the sons of men.
>
> I was in the world and received of my Father, and the works of him were plainly manifest.

The same will be true of you and me—to a much lesser degree. The Father will give you whatever portion of His power necessary to perform your mortal mission.

In addition to what He revealed above about His being "the true light that lighteth every man that cometh into the world," the power of the Savior and the scope of His influence is outlined throughout scripture but concisely recorded in Doctrine and Covenants 88:6–13:

> He that ascended up on high, as also he descended below all things, in that he comprehended all things, that he might be in all and through all things, the light of truth;
>
> Which truth shineth. This is the light of Christ. As also he is in the sun, and the light of the sun, and the power thereof by which it was made.
>
> As also he is in the moon, and is the light of the moon, and the power thereof by which it was made;
>
> As also the light of the stars, and the power thereof by which they were made;
>
> And the earth also, and the power thereof, even the earth upon which you stand.
>
> And the light which shineth, which giveth you light, is through him who enlighteneth your eyes, which is the same light that quickeneth your understandings;
>
> Which light proceedeth forth from the presence of God to fill the immensity of space—
>
> The light which is in all things, which giveth life to all things, which is the law by which all things are governed,

> even the power of God who sitteth upon his throne, who is in the bosom of eternity, who is in the midst of all things.

The depth of this doctrine goes far beyond the scope of this book, so we will outline only the four described powers of the light of Christ:

1. It is a creative power (verses 6–10)
2. It is an enlightening power (verses 11–12)
3. It is a life-giving power (verse 13)
4. It is a governing power (verse 13)

Explaining to the early Saints why they could trust Him to lead them from the then civilized region of New York to "the Ohio"—definitely the wild frontier—the Savior said:

> Thus saith the Lord your God, even Jesus Christ, the Great I Am, Alpha and Omega, the beginning and the end, the same which looked upon the wide expanse of eternity, and all the seraphic hosts of heaven, before the world was made;
>
> The same which knoweth all things, for all things are present before mine eyes;
>
> I am the same which spake, and the world was made, and all things came by me.
>
> I am the same which have taken the Zion of Enoch into mine own bosom; and verily, I say, even as many as have believed in my name, for I am Christ, and in mine own name, by the virtue of the blood which I have spilt, have I pleaded before the Father for them.
>
> But behold, the residue of the wicked have I kept in chains of darkness until the judgment of the great day, which shall come at the end of the earth;
>
> And even so will I cause the wicked to be kept, that will not hear my voice but harden their hearts, and wo, wo, wo, is their doom.

> But behold, verily, verily, I say unto you that mine eyes are upon you. I am in your midst and ye cannot see me;
>
> But the day soon cometh that ye shall see me, and know that I am; for the veil of darkness shall soon be rent, and he that is not purified shall not abide the day.
>
> Wherefore, gird up your loins and be prepared. Behold, the kingdom is yours, and the enemy shall not overcome. (D&C 38:1–9)

Contained in those verses is the assurance that He has all power, He was involved in what was happening to them on a daily basis, that He controls the wicked, and that their ever-present enemies would not overcome them. Those same promises are applied to each of us.

The Savior explains His role as our Advocate with the Father:

> Listen to him who is the advocate with the Father, who is pleading your cause before him—
>
> Saying: Father, behold the sufferings and death of him who did no sin, in whom thou wast well pleased; behold the blood of thy Son which was shed, the blood of him whom thou gavest that thyself might be glorified;
>
> Wherefore, Father, spare these my brethren that believe on my name, that they may come unto me and have everlasting life. (D&C 45:3–5, you will want to read verse 1–15)

In Section 20, also known as the constitutional doctrine, organization, and government of His Church, the Lord revealed:

> By these things [the Book of Mormon and later the restoration scriptures] we know that there is a God in heaven, who is infinite and eternal, from everlasting to everlasting the same unchangeable God, the framer of heaven and earth, and all things which are in them;
>
> And that he created man, male and female, after his own image and in his own likeness, created he them;

> And gave unto them commandments that they should love and serve him, the only living and true God, and that he should be the only being whom they should worship.
>
> But by the transgression of these holy laws man became sensual and devilish, and became fallen man.
>
> Wherefore, the Almighty God gave his Only Begotten Son, as it is written in those scriptures which have been given of him.
>
> He suffered temptations but gave no heed unto them.
>
> He was crucified, died, and rose again the third day;
>
> And ascended into heaven, to sit down on the right hand of the Father, to reign with almighty power according to the will of the Father;
>
> That as many as would believe and be baptized in his holy name, and endure in faith to the end, should be saved—
>
> Not only those who believed after he came in the meridian of time, in the flesh, but all those from the beginning, even as many as were before he came, who believed in the words of the holy prophets, who spake as they were inspired by the gift of the Holy Ghost, who truly testified of him in all things, should have eternal life,
>
> As well as those who should come after, who should believe in the gifts and callings of God by the Holy Ghost, which beareth record of the Father and of the Son;
>
> Which Father, Son, and Holy Ghost are one God, infinite and eternal, without end. Amen. (D&C 20:17–28)

For your edification and the consoling of all those you meet, seek to understand what Alma taught:

> And he shall go forth, *suffering pains and afflictions and temptations of every kind*; and this that the word might be fulfilled which saith he will take upon him the pains and the sicknesses of his people.

> And he will take upon him death, that he may loose the bands of death which bind his people; and he will take upon him *their infirmities*, that his bowels may be filled with mercy, according to the flesh, that he may know according to the flesh *how to succor his people according to their infirmities.*
>
> Now the Spirit knoweth all things; nevertheless the Son of God suffereth according to the flesh that *he might take upon him the sins of his people*, that he might blot out their transgressions according to the power of his deliverance; and now behold, this is the testimony which is in me. (Alma 7:11–13, emphasis added)

No wonder that Alma said: "For behold, I say unto you there be many things to come; and behold, there is one thing which is of more importance than they all—for behold, the time is not far distant that the Redeemer liveth and cometh among his people" (Alma 7:7).

It would take volumes to fully outline the roles, the involvement, and the closeness that the Savior has for us. However, this invitation sets the stage for our study of some of the key doctrine of the Doctrine and Covenants: "Learn of me, and listen to my words; walk in the meekness of my Spirit, and you shall have peace in me" (D&C 19:23).

As one final contrast between what came from Christian scholars debating (without priesthood power or revelation) the nature of God and Christ at the Council of Nicaea, read what fifteen prophets, seers, and revelators said of Christ in our day:

The Living Christ: The Testimony of the Apostles of The Church of Jesus Christ of Latter-day Saints

> As we commemorate the birth of Jesus Christ two millennia ago, we offer our testimony of the reality of His matchless life and the infinite virtue of His great atoning sacrifice. None other has had so profound an influence upon all who have lived and will yet live upon the earth.

He was the Great Jehovah of the Old Testament, the Messiah of the New. Under the direction of His Father, He was the creator of the earth. "All things were made by him; and without him was not any thing made that was made" (John 1:3). Though sinless, He was baptized to fulfill all righteousness. He "went about doing good" (Acts 10:38), yet was despised for it. His gospel was a message of peace and goodwill. He entreated all to follow His example. He walked the roads of Palestine, healing the sick, causing the blind to see, and raising the dead. He taught the truths of eternity, the reality of our premortal existence, the purpose of our life on earth, and the potential for the sons and daughters of God in the life to come.

He instituted the sacrament as a reminder of His great atoning sacrifice. He was arrested and condemned on spurious charges, convicted to satisfy a mob, and sentenced to die on Calvary's cross. He gave His life to atone for the sins of all mankind. His was a great vicarious gift in behalf of all who would ever live upon the earth.

We solemnly testify that His life, which is central to all human history, neither began in Bethlehem nor concluded on Calvary. He was the Firstborn of the Father, the Only Begotten Son in the flesh, the Redeemer of the world. He rose from the grave to "become the firstfruits of them that slept" (1 Corinthians 15:20). As Risen Lord, He visited among those He had loved in life. He also ministered among His "other sheep" (John 10:16) in ancient America. In the modern world, He and His Father appeared to the boy Joseph Smith, ushering in the long-promised "dispensation of the fulness of times" (Ephesians 1:10).

Of the Living Christ, the Prophet Joseph wrote: "His eyes were as a flame of fire; the hair of his head was white like the pure snow; his countenance shone above the brightness of the sun; and his voice was as the sound of the rushing of great waters, even the voice of Jehovah, saying:

"I am the first and the last; I am he who liveth, I am he who was slain; I am your advocate with the Father" (D&C 110:3–4).

Of Him the Prophet also declared: "And now, after the many testimonies which have been given of him, this is the testimony, last of all, which we give of him: That he lives!

"For we saw him, even on the right hand of God; and we heard the voice bearing record that he is the Only Begotten of the Father—

"That by him, and through him, and of him, the worlds are and were created, and the inhabitants thereof are begotten sons and daughters unto God" (D&C 76:22–24).

We declare in words of solemnity that His priesthood and His Church have been restored upon the earth— "built upon the foundation of . . . apostles and prophets, Jesus Christ himself being the chief corner stone" (Ephesians 2:20).

We testify that He will someday return to earth. "And the glory of the Lord shall be revealed, and all flesh shall see it together" (Isaiah 40:5). He will rule as King of Kings and reign as Lord of Lords, and every knee shall bend and every tongue shall speak in worship before Him. Each of us will stand to be judged of Him according to our works and the desires of our hearts.

We bear testimony, as His duly ordained Apostles— that Jesus is the Living Christ, the immortal Son of God. He is the great King Immanuel, who stands today on the right hand of His Father. He is the light, the life, and the hope of the world. His way is the path that leads to happiness in this life and eternal life in the world to come. God be thanked for the matchless gift of His divine Son.

The First Presidency
Quorum of the Twelve Apostles
January 1, 2000

The Plan of Salvation

God's Great Plan for the Future of His Children

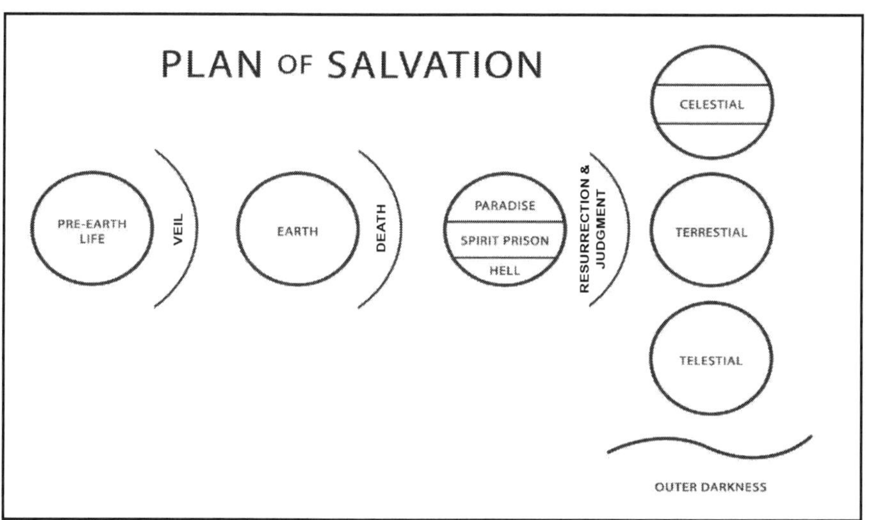

Most Latter-day Saints will be familiar with the above schematic drawing representing the plan of salvation. If you are a lifelong member of the Church, you may ask: "Doesn't everyone know about this?" The answer, for a person who is not a member of the Church, is a new convert, or has never seriously studied what the Church teaches, is "NO."

Let's take a minute and analyze what you are taking to the world. You are not just taking "a little" to add to their understanding—you are taking a huge amount.

What does the restored gospel add?

First, although taught in the Bible, the "Christian World" knows nothing about the pre-mortal existence. From our understanding of the pre-earth life, we know that we are the literal spirit offspring of exalted Parents. Without that understanding, the Christian world knows nothing about the literal parent/child relationship of humans to God.

Although the war in heaven is described by John in the Book of Revelation (see Revelation 12:7–9), without a more complete knowledge of the great council in heaven and Lucifer's counterplan, the Christian world knows nothing about who Satan truly is and what the war in heaven was about.

They know nothing about the veil of forgetfulness and its purpose in separating us from the knowledge of our pre-earth life.

From our drawing of the plan of salvation, we must erase the pre-earth life and the veil.

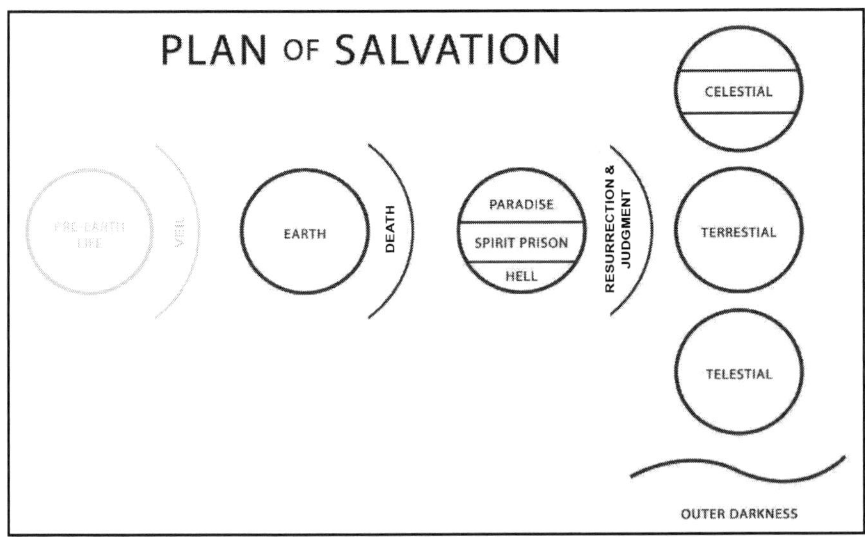

Second, Christians have only a vague idea of the total purpose of mortality. It is through the scriptures of the restoration that we understand that earth life is a probationary time designed as a time to prepare to meet God.

Many do not understand the necessity of ordinances, or even what they are, or that they are required for re-entrance into the presence of God. They either do not know about or deny the eternity of the marriage and family relationship.

They either know nothing about or deny the need for priesthood, Church organization, revelation, prophets and apostles, and vicarious work for the dead.

From our drawing of the plan of salvation, we must erase about 90% of the circle representing earth life.

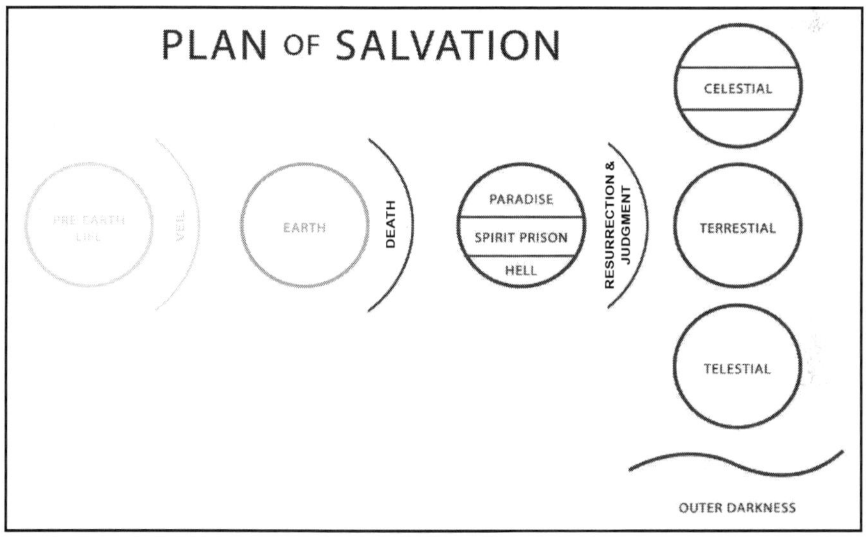

Third, without the added insight of the restored gospel, Christians understand very little about the purpose of death. Often Christians look upon death as a terrible tragedy. Later we will shed a great deal of light on death as a welcome graduation from earth life into a much better place.

In keeping with our analysis of the schematic of the Plan of Salvation, we must erase the line representing death.

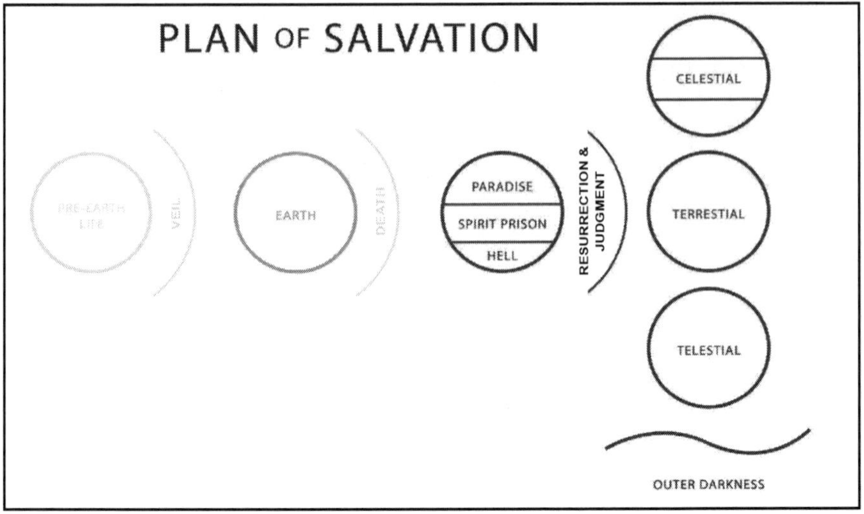

Fourth, without the knowledge revealed in the restoration, Christians know nothing about the post-mortal spirit world, what is done there, and what the divisions are. They don't know about the preaching of the gospel to all who did not hear or embrace or understand it here on earth. It is taught in 1 Peter 3:18–20; 4:6 but it is not understood.

Now we must erase the circle representing the post-earth spirit world.

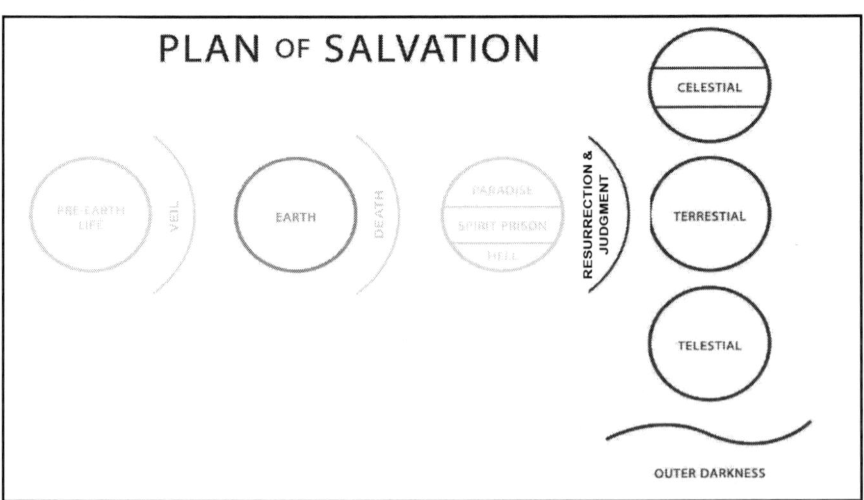

Fifth, Christians know very little about the resurrection. When will it occur? Is there more than one time? What is the timing when the different classes of people will be resurrected? What about resurrection during the Millennium? And what is the criteria for the different resurrections? All of which will be discussed in detail later in this book.

They know very little about the final judgment. When will it occur? What are the criteria that we will be judged by? Who will judge us? And what are the possible outcomes of the judgment?

Now we must erase the line representing resurrection and judgment because of the incompleteness of the understanding by the vast body of Christians.

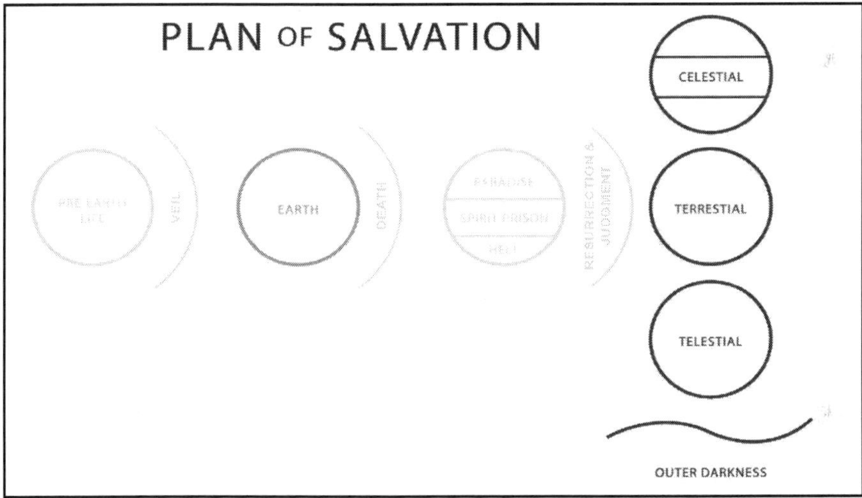

Sixth, Christians know nothing about the three degrees of glory although it is taught in the Bible. They will know nothing about the divisions in the celestial kingdom. Their understanding of a heaven and a hell is really inaccurate.

Now the circles representing the three degrees of glory and outer darkness must be erased because they do not understand or accept them.

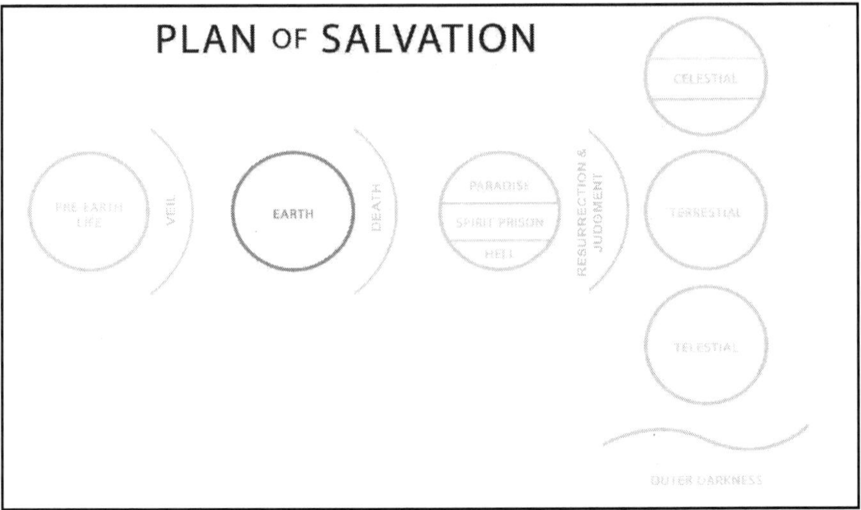

Seventh, although the ultimate destiny of mankind is to become like God, the whole of Christianity rejects the possible exaltation of man.

So, you can clearly see what you are taking to the people of the world, look at the two schematic representation of the Plan of Salvation as restored through the Prophet Joseph Smith, and what has been lost since Christ taught the plan in its fullness while He was on earth.

You are commissioned to take the fullness of the restored gospel to the world. Let's make sure you are well armed and prepared to fulfill your divine commission to "take the world his truth."

What they know . . .

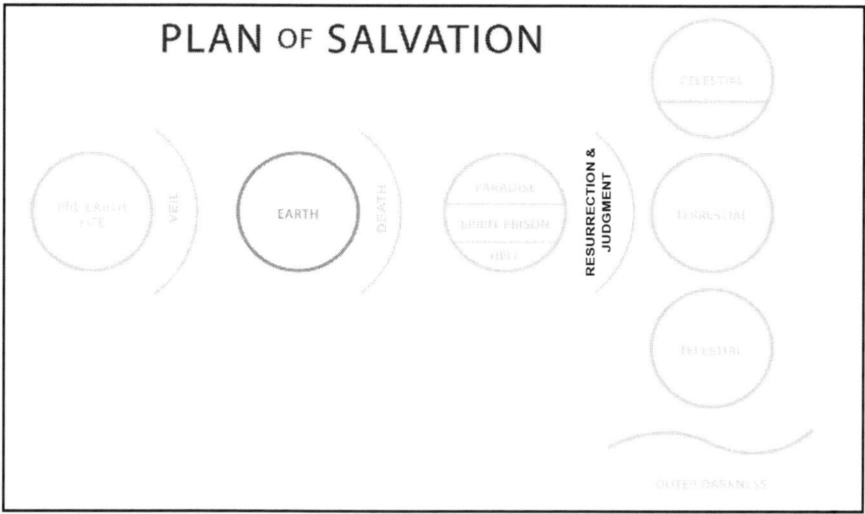

What we know . . .

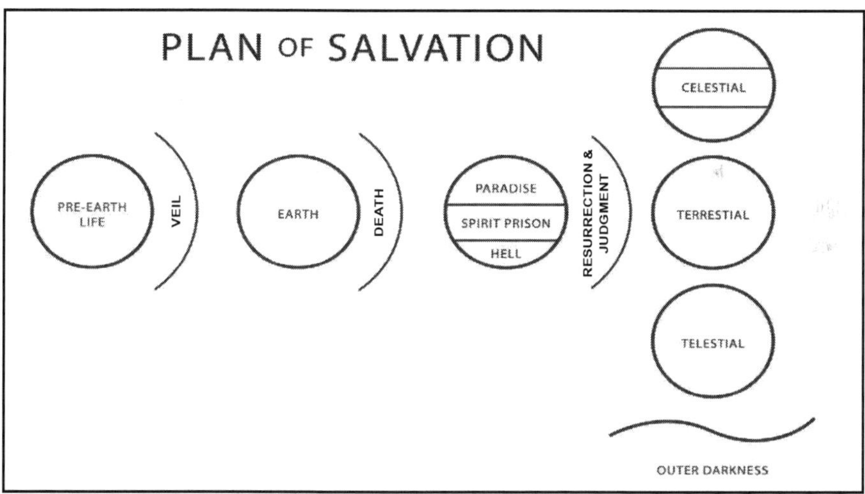

. . . "Take the world his truth."

Chapter 1

First Vision—Godhead

When the great God of Heaven set His hand the second time to restore the gospel—for the last time—He started with the revelation of the Godhead. Although the First Vision is not one of the numbered 138 sections in the Doctrine and Covenants, it is the foundation upon which the entire restoration is based. Make sure you read and re-read Joseph Smith History 1:11–20 for the account of the First Vision in Joseph Smith's own words.

If the account of the First Vision is not true, then the entire restoration crumbles as a building without a solid foundation. If the First Vision is true, then it stands to reason that Joseph Smith is a prophet and that the Book of Mormon translated by him, and the revelations received through him, are from God and are as much scripture as anything written in the Bible.

What do we learn from the First Vision? Joseph Smith's experience refuted the prevalent Christian teaching that revelation had ceased, that the heavens were sealed, and that God and angels no longer appeared to men on earth.

Joseph learned in a near-death experience that Satan is real and has an amazing amount of power. Joseph saw that Satan will do everything in his power to stop the restoration from happening and spreading throughout the world.

Many of the early leaders taught that the "pillar of light" was the Holy Ghost descending upon young Joseph. It dispelled the powers of darkness and prepared Joseph to receive the greatest vision since the resurrection of the Savior.

The appearance of the Father and the Son refuted the idea that God, Christ, and the Holy Ghost are all combined into one being. Whether Joseph realized that God had a body of flesh and bones at that time, we do not know, but we do know that Joseph learned that God had created man in His own image and that the Father and the Son were separate beings.

Joseph learned that God knew him when He called Joseph by his first name. Joseph also learned that he could talk to God and Christ like one man speaks to another. He now knew that he could ask God a question and get a straight answer (i.e. which church was right and which he should join).

Joseph learned that the true church of Christ was not on the earth at that time but that he would be instrumental in restoring the truth to the earth.

This is the first and the most important factor in you becoming a powerful instrument in the hands of God to share His gospel to His spirit children throughout the earth. You must have a rock-solid testimony that the First Vision actually happened. Don't make the mistake of believing that you can rely upon your parents' testimony, or the bishop's, or even the President of the Church's testimony. Your testimony fired by personal confirming inspiration will kindle the flame in countless others.

You do not have to have the same experience as Joseph Smith to be able to testify about Joseph's experience with the Godhead, but you do need the Holy Ghost to bear witness to you that what Joseph Smith reported is true. How can you get that testimony or strengthen the testimony you have? Moroni gave the formula in a scripture you are very familiar with:

> Behold, I would exhort you that when ye shall read these things, if it be wisdom in God that ye should read them, that ye would remember how merciful the Lord hath been unto the children of men, from the creation of Adam even

> down until the time that ye shall receive these things, and ponder it in your hearts.
>
> And when ye shall receive these things, I would exhort you that ye would ask God, the Eternal Father, in the name of Christ, if these things are not true; and if ye shall ask with a sincere heart, with real intent, having faith in Christ, he will manifest the truth of it unto you, by the power of the Holy Ghost.
>
> And by the power of the Holy Ghost ye may know the truth of all things. (Moroni 10:3–5)

You are going to challenge investigators to get their own testimony that the First Vision is true and that Joseph Smith is a prophet. How can you expect them to do something you haven't done? If your testimony needs strengthening (and all of our testimonies can be stronger!), then start now studying, praying, and learning to recognize the "still small voice" and the promptings of the Spirit testifying that what you are going to be teaching really is true.

Once you get that witness, don't stop there. Continue studying, praying, and living the gospel until you have a perfect knowledge that all the fiery darts of the adversary cannot destroy. A living, vibrant testimony renewed daily is far better than a vision or revelation received years before but never built upon. Keep growing.

For your investigators (or others you will teach):

Whether your investigators are hearing the account of the First Vision for the first time or the fiftieth time, they still must humble themselves and ask the Lord for a manifestation that what you have testified of is true. If they are not willing to ask, they have placed an insurmountable roadblock in their way of gaining a testimony. James, the ancient apostle, said: "Ye have not, because ye ask not" (James 4:2). Sometimes investigators (usually not sincere in wanting to know if the gospel has been restored), ask in the negative: "Heavenly Father this couldn't possibly be true!" James continues: "Ye ask, and receive not, because ye ask amiss" (James 4:3).The key is to ask for a confirmation, not a rebuttal.

It may surprise you (it certainly surprised me!) to learn that many devout Christians do not believe that God will answer their prayers by giving them an answer through revelation. Read with them James 1:5–6—the very verses which motivated young Joseph Smith to inquire of the Lord.

Be aware that, either knowingly or unconsciously, their ministers, family, or friends will do all in their power to prevent them from seriously investigating. Perhaps reminding them of what Joseph's experience was with "the powers of darkness" (see Joseph Smith History 1:20) will put them on guard of what will (to one degree or another) happen to them.

If the Spirit has been there during your discussion of the First Vision, it would greatly benefit your investigators if you would warn them that they could very possibly experience some satanic attacks to dissuade them from getting their own testimony. Remind them what Mormon taught that "the devil is an enemy unto God, and fighteth against him continually" (Moroni 7:12).

If you fail to warn them, they may only crack open the door and tell you to go away the next time you visit because their lives have been in total chaos. Whereas if you warn them before you leave, they may swing open the door and pull you in, testifying that you must be prophets since the satanic attacks you forewarned them about actually happened.

Far too often otherwise serious investigators will turn to the internet to see what people are saying about the Church. Be forewarned that much of what is on the internet is negative and written by anti-Mormons or apostate Mormons specifically designed to destroy the faith of people and prevent them from joining the Church.

You must realize and help them understand that God has chosen to provide the indisputable witness of the truthfulness of the gospel—a personal testimony by the Holy Ghost. Then even if you or your investigator do not know how to answer every challenge the anti's throw against you and the Church, that undeniable witness from God, Himself, should provide sufficient evidence to override all other attacks.

Prepare now to answer their probing question: "How do you know that the First Vision actually happened?" Can you envision a more powerful response than: "God has revealed it to me by the power of the Holy Ghost. I therefore have an unshakable testimony that what Joseph Smith recorded really did happen."

Chapter 2

Revelation—Line upon Line

Almost every section of the Doctrine and Covenants comes as a result of Joseph Smith and the early leaders of the Church asking questions. Some Latter-day Saints expect that Joseph Smith would have a full understanding of the gospel when he came out of the Sacred Grove.

Revelation comes a little bit at a time as we receive and live by what has been revealed. The Lord said: "And I give unto you a commandment, that ye shall forsake all evil and cleave unto all good, that ye shall live by every word which proceedeth forth out of the mouth of God.

For he will give unto the faithful line upon line, precept upon precept; and I will try you and prove you herewith" (D&C 98:11–12).

You must learn to ask for, receive, and act upon revelation as part of becoming a powerful missionary. It would be helpful if you take a big step back and ask yourself: "What do I know I am doing or not doing that would cause the Spirit to withdraw from me?" If you have been deceived into believing that you are near perfect (one of Satan's tactics) and don't need to repent, the Lord has promised: "Verily I say unto you, my servant [put your name in here], that you are clean, but not all; repent, therefore, of those things which are not pleasing in my sight, saith the Lord, for the Lord will show them unto you" (D&C 66:3).

As you eliminate the roadblocks to revelation and incorporate those actions which invite the Spirit, you will begin to experience what the Lord told Hyrum Smith as he was anxious to share the gospel—even before the Church was restored:

> And now, verily, verily, I say unto thee, put your trust in that Spirit which leadeth to do good—yea, to do justly, to walk humbly, to judge righteously; and this is my Spirit.
>
> Verily, verily, I say unto you, I will impart unto you of my Spirit, which shall enlighten your mind, which shall fill your soul with joy;
>
> And then shall ye know, or by this shall you know, all things whatsoever you desire of me, which are pertaining unto things of righteousness, in faith believing in me that you shall receive. (D&C 11:12–14)

Read those three verses carefully. The more you respond to the promptings of the Spirit, the easier it will be to develop into a Christlike person and the wider the gates to celestial knowledge will be. Along the way you will find you can think faster on your feet, remember more of what you have learned, and bask in the joy that comes with knowing that God is tutoring you and helping you become an instrument in His hands.

There are two scriptures that can help eliminate fear that Satan throws in your face when you are asked difficult questions: "Neither take ye thought beforehand what ye shall say; but *treasure up in your minds continually the words of life*, and it shall be given you in the very hour that portion that shall be meted unto every man" (D&C 84:85, emphasis added).

Note what you have to do to qualify for that kind of revelatory assistance: "Treasure up in your minds continually the words of life." If you don't have one yet, establish a daily time to study the scriptures and talks by General Authorities. Make it a goal to read the Book of Mormon multiple times before your mission. Develop a lifelong practice of reading and re-reading the Book of Mormon.

The second scripture is even more encouraging:

> Therefore, verily I say unto you, lift up your voices unto this people; speak the thoughts that I shall put into your hearts, and you shall not be confounded before men;
>
> For it shall be given you in the very hour, yea, *in the very moment*, what ye shall say.
>
> But a commandment I give unto you, that ye shall declare whatsoever thing ye declare in my name, in solemnity of heart, in the spirit of meekness, in all things.
>
> And I give unto you this promise, that inasmuch as ye do this the Holy Ghost shall be shed forth in bearing record unto all things whatsoever ye shall say. (D&C 100:5–8, emphasis added)

The Lord promises that He will give you "in the very moment" what you are to say as you preach the gospel. But equally as important is the promise that the Lord will send the Holy Ghost to testify of the truthfulness of what you are preaching. Don't ever get the mistaken idea that you are alone on your mission. In fact, it isn't "*your* mission"—it is the Savior's mission that you are privileged to participate in.

Sometimes you will be confronted with questions that you do not know how to answer. Don't be afraid to say: "That is a really good question. I don't know the answer to it. But I will find the answer and we can discuss it next time we meet."Then go to your apartment and ask the Lord to lead you to the answer. He promised: "If thou shalt ask, thou shalt receive revelation upon revelation, knowledge upon knowledge, that thou mayest know the mysteries and peaceable things—that which bringeth joy, that which bringeth life eternal" (D&C 42:61).

Be aware that there many ways the Lord reveals truths to you as the missionary and to your investigators also.

Recognizing How the Spirit Impacts You—

1. Gives feelings of love, joy, peace, patience, meekness, gentleness, faith, and hope (D&C 6:23, D&C 11:12–14; Romans 15:13; Galatians 5:22–23)
2. Gives ideas in the mind and feeling sin the heart (D&C 8:2–3)
3. Occupies the mind and presses on the feelings (D&C 128:1)
4. Helps scriptures have strong effect (Joseph Smith—History 1:11–12)
5. Gives good feelings to teach if something is true (D&C 9:8–9)
6. Enlightens the mind (Alma 32:28; D&C 6:14–15; 1 Corinthians 2:9–11)
7. Replaces darkness with light (Alma 19:6)
8. Strengthens the desire to avoid evil and obey the commandments (Mosiah 5:2–5)
9. Teaches truth and brings all things to remembrance (John 14:26)
10. Gives feelings of peace and comfort—(John 14:27)
11. Guides to truth and shows things to come (John 16:13)
12. Reveals truth (Moroni 10:5)
13. Guides and protects from deception (D&C 45:57)
14. Glorifies and bears record of God the Father and Jesus Christ (2 Nephi 31:18; D&C 20:27; John 16:14)
15. Guides the words of humble teachers (D&C 42:16; 84:85; 100:5–8; Luke 12:11–12)
16. Recognized and corrects sin (John 16:8)

17. Gives gifts of the Spirit (Moroni 10:8–17; D&C 46:8–26; 1 Corinthians 12)
18. Helps to perceive or discern the thoughts of others (Alma 10:17; Alma 12:3; Alma 18:16, 20, 32, 35; D&C 63:41)
19. Tells what to pray for (Romans 8:26; 3 Nephi 19:24; D&C 46:28, 30; D&C 50:29–30)
20. Tells what to do (1 Nephi 4:6; 2 Nephi 32:1–5; D&C 28:15; Helaman 5:18)
21. Teaches where to go (D&C 79:2; Helaman 5:18)
22. Helps the righteous speak with power and authority (1 Nephi 10:22; Alma 18:35)
23. Testifies of the truth (D&C 21:9; 100:8; John 15:26)
24. Sanctifies and brings remission of sins (2 Nephi 31:17; Alma 13:12; 3 Nephi 27:20)
25. Carries truth unto the heart of the listener (1 Nephi 2:16–17; 2 Nephi 33:1; Alma 24:8)
26. Enhances skills and abilities (1 Nephi 1:1–3; Exodus 31:3–5)
27. Constrains [impels forward] or restrains [holds back] (1 Nephi 7:15; 2 Nephi 28:1; 32:7; Alma 14:11; Mormon 3:16; Ether 12:2)
28. Edifies both teacher and students (D&C 50:13–22)
29. Gives comfort (D&C 88:3; John 14:26)
30. Helps understand scriptures like never before (Joseph Smith—History 1:74)

(Adapted from *Preach My Gospel* [2004], 96–97)

The more familiar you become to the promptings of the Spirit the easier it will be for you to help your investigators recognize when the Spirit is working with them. As you strengthen your trust in the Lord and His promises, the easier it will be for you to encourage and reassure your investigators that revelations are real and that one needn't be a prophet or called leader in order for the Lord to reveal His will to them.

For your investigators:

Because most churches do not believe in continuing revelation, you may well experience some serious challenges as you teach that revelation continues in our days and is available to them. Consider that the Lord has given an open invitation to everyone: "Ask, and it shall be given you; seek, and ye shall find; knock, and it shall be opened unto you: For *every one* that asketh receiveth; and he that seeketh findeth; and to him that knocketh it shall be opened" (Matthew 7:7–8, emphasis added).

Remember, the invitation to "ask" with the promise that "everyone" will receive is not exclusively Mormon doctrine.

In an effort to confuse people, ministers and others will often mock at receiving answers to sincere prayers by feelings we experience. Too often skeptics will say: "Oh you just want it to be true so you convince yourself that you have had a revelation!"

In explaining the parable of the sower and the seed in Matthew 13, the Lord described this kind of undermining by the adversary:

> But he that received the seed into stony places, the same is he that heareth the word, and anon with joy receiveth it;
>
> Yet hath he not root in himself, but dureth for a while: for when tribulation or persecution ariseth because of the word, by and by he is offended. (Matthew 13:20–21)

Sharing your personal experience in receiving inspiration or revelation often helps investigators bolster the courage to continue asking and to fend off the mocking and pointing finger of scorn that follows when they've successfully received a witness. Teach them to expect to receive revelation!

Chapter 3

The Family

Considering the hundreds of things the Lord could reveal first, it certainly will come as a surprise to the world that He chose to reveal the importance of the family. Almost seven years before the Church was restored, Moroni, now a resurrected being, appeared to Joseph Smith. Just so you know, Section 1 (the Lord's Preface) and Section 133 (the Appendix) were revealed a year and a half after the Church was restored. The first chronological section is #2.

Section 2 is very short and records only a small portion of what the Angel Moroni told Joseph Smith on the night of September 21–22, 1823. Moroni told Joseph Smith that Elijah the Prophet (who was translated) was to visit him and "reveal" the priesthood. We will discuss later that John the Baptist "restored" the Aaronic Priesthood and Peter, James, and John "restored" the Melchizedek Priesthood.

What did Elijah "reveal"? In Doctrine and Covenants 110:13–16, the fulfillment of Elijah's promised visit is recorded:

> After this vision had closed, another great and glorious vision burst upon us; for Elijah the prophet, who was taken to heaven without tasting death, stood before us, and said:
>
> Behold, the time has fully come, which was spoken of by the mouth of Malachi—testifying that he [Elijah] should

> be sent, before the great and dreadful day of the Lord come—
>
> To turn the hearts of the fathers to the children, and the children to the fathers, lest the whole earth be smitten with a curse—
>
> Therefore, the keys of this dispensation are committed into your hands; and by this ye may know that the great and dreadful day of the Lord is near, even at the doors.

In the next chapter, we will discuss God's warning about Satan, his tactics, and how to overcome his influence. Satan who is called "an enemy to God" (see Mosiah 16:5) realized that his efforts to stop the creation of the earth had failed. Thus, there was a physical earth where the sons and daughters of God could get physical bodies and learn what they needed to progress eventually becoming like God. Satan sought to destroy mankind by tempting Eve to partake of the fruit of the tree of knowledge of good and evil contrary to God's command: ". . . he sought also to beguile Eve, for he knew not the mind of God, wherefore he sought to destroy the world" (Moses 4:6).

Failing also to prevent the birth of God's spirit children to the now mortal Adam and Eve, Satan tried to prevent the Savior growing to maturity by inspiring Herod to have all little children killed (see Matthew 2).Satan also did all in his power to keep the Savior from living the perfect life thus disqualifying Him from being worthy to perform the Infinite Atonement (see Matthew 4:1–11 for the account of the temptations of the Savior). Perhaps believing if he (Satan) could cause the death of Jesus, he could prevent His resurrection and therefore would be able to hold all of humanity subject to his eternal misery. Note what Jacob taught:

> Wherefore, it must needs be an infinite atonement—save it should be an infinite atonement this corruption could not put on incorruption. Wherefore, the first judgment which came upon man must needs have remained to an endless duration. And if so, this flesh must have laid down to rot and to crumble to its mother earth, to rise no more.

> O the wisdom of God, his mercy and grace! For behold, if the flesh should rise no more our spirits must become subject to that angel who fell from before the presence of the Eternal God, and became the devil, to rise no more.
>
> And our spirits must have become like unto him, and we become devils, angels to a devil, to be shut out from the presence of our God, and to remain with the father of lies, in misery, like unto himself" (2 Nephi 9:7–9).

Satan really is the eternal loser! Everything he tries seems to backfire in his face. Having failed to destroy the pillars of the plan of salvation (i.e. the Creation, the Fall, Christ's Atonement, and the Resurrection), he turned his evil efforts on trying to destroy us individually.

He knows that only temple married couples can inherit the highest degree of the celestial kingdom (see D&C 131:1–4—to be discussed in a later chapter). He knows that "Families Can Be Together Forever" isn't just a cutesy slogan but an eternal reality. Therefore, his unrelenting efforts are now focused on destroying marriages and families.

As you enter the mission field, you will see how miserably effective Satan is in destroying marriages. In fact, even among the Latter-day Saints, the divorce rate is out of control. The dissolution of the marriage covenant throws the family into disarray. Almost every evil in today's world can be traced to the destruction of the family.

Familiarize yourself with "The Family: A Proclamation to the World" that the First Presidency and Quorum of the Twelve Apostles published in 1995. Since that proclamation was sent to the world, same-sex marriages have been legalized, gay and lesbians have been given full marital rights, atheists have succeeded in pushing their agenda through liberal courts to deny Christians the rights to celebrate Christmas or Easter (claiming the imposing of religion on them), and a whole host of such evidences that Satan is having his way with modern man.

Your voice supporting marriage between a man and a woman must be loud, clear, and unmistakable. Are you likely to run into satanic opposition? No doubt you will. However, under the influence of the Spirit you will know how and what to say in defense of marriage and the family. Those who are wandering in the wilderness surrounded by the mists of darkness mentioned in Lehi's dream (see 1 Nephi 8) will welcome the sure light you are holding up. That light is the doctrine of Christ. He said to the Nephites: "Therefore, hold up your light that it may shine unto the world. Behold I am the light which ye shall hold up—that which ye have seen me do" (3 Nephi 18:24).

Even among a growing number of Latter-day Saints, the very purpose of marriage is unknown or willfully disregarded. Here is what the Lord told Joseph Smith about marriage:

> And again, verily I say unto you, that whoso forbiddeth to marry is not ordained of God, for marriage is ordained of God unto man.
>
> Wherefore, it is lawful that he should have one wife, and they twain shall be one flesh, and all this that the earth might answer the end of its creation;
>
> And that it might be filled with the measure of man, according to his creation before the world was made. (D&C 49:15–17)

This will be discussed further in the chapter on marriage and family

You will undoubtedly experience opposition among some young married Latter-day Saint couples who believe marriage is strictly to legitimize sexual relations. You must understand that when you stand for what the Lord has revealed, you become a primary target for the devil and his angels.

For your investigators:

Given the way the lawmakers are attempting to overturn the commands of God, it is inevitable that you will encounter dissident voices. Isaiah saw our day and how arrogant people would try to turn God's commandments upside down. He wrote:

> Woe unto them that seek deep to hide their counsel from the Lord, and their works are in the dark, and they say, Who seeth us? and who knoweth us?

> Surely your turning of things upside down shall be esteemed as the potter's clay: for shall the work say of him that made it, He made me not? or shall the thing framed say of him that framed it, He had no understanding? (Isaiah 29:15–16)

Earlier in his writings, Isaiah had recorded this warning:

> Woe unto them that call evil good, and good evil; that put darkness for light, and light for darkness; that put bitter for sweet, and sweet for bitter!
>
> Woe unto them that are wise in their own eyes, and prudent in their own sight! (Isaiah 5:20–21)

Surely we live in a day when these prophecies are being fulfilled. Remind your investigators that from the very beginning of mankind on this earth, the Lord ordained marriage as His prescribed unit of society. He said:

> And the Lord God caused a deep sleep to fall upon Adam, and he slept: and he took one of his ribs, and closed up the flesh instead thereof;
>
> And the rib, which the Lord God had taken from man, made he a woman, and brought her unto the man.
>
> And Adam said, This is now bone of my bones, and flesh of my flesh: she shall be called Woman, because she was taken out of Man.
>
> Therefore shall a man leave his father and his mother, and *shall cleave unto his wife*: and they shall be one flesh. (Genesis 2:21–24, emphasis added)

From the time that God brought the woman to Adam, she is referred to as his wife. We will visit this topic again when we discuss marriage.

It would be wise for you to carry (in your scriptures) a copy of "The Family: A Proclamation to the World." The second to last paragraph reads as follows:

> We warn that individuals who violate covenants of chastity, who abuse spouse or offspring, or who fail to fulfill family responsibilities will one day stand accountable before God. Further, we warn that the disintegration of the family will bring upon the individuals, communities, and nations the calamities foretold by ancient and modern prophets.

It is also instructive to note that of all the titles God could choose to be addressed by, "Father" is the one He chose. Wisdom would dictate that a discussion of Mother in Heaven be avoided and saved for a later time when the foundation has been firmly laid for the doctrine that leads up to such a discussion. Far too many missionaries (from my experience) want to jump immediately to the "rafter" doctrine of the godship of man and Mother in Heaven, etc. before laying a foundation and stud walls to support that doctrine. You will lose a lot of otherwise golden investigators if you try to give them "meat before milk" (i.e. deep doctrine before foundational doctrine).

The Lord gave this stern warning even before the Church was restored: "And I command you that you preach naught but repentance, and show not these things unto the world until it is wisdom in me. For they cannot bear meat now, but milk they must receive; wherefore, they must not know these things, lest they perish" (D&C 19:21–22).

Don't make the mistake of trying to teach too much too fast. Start with the basics and wait for them to establish a firm foundation. Soon enough they will want to know more—probably not while you are teaching them.

Chapter 4

Satan's Attempts to Destroy

Beginning at the First Vision, Satan's influences have been noted. However, even before the Church was restored, a number of revelations are devoted to identifying and overcoming Satan's influence.

In Section 3, the Lord is chastising Joseph Smith for giving into Martin Harris who repeatedly asked to take the 116 manuscript pages of the Book of Mormon (containing the Book of Lehi) to show to his wife and several others. We would be wise to identify when people (friends, family, or others) attempt to influence us to do what we know is wrong and contrary to the Lord's will.

Although the Lord had made provisions for this loss 2,500 years earlier (see 1 Nephi 9:5–6), this incident is a stern warning to all of us not to yield to the persuasions of men. You may think this was a small issue but consider that Joseph's choice cost the entire world access to a book of scripture from 1830 to the Second Coming.

Not unlike Joseph Smith, some of us have made serious mistakes and wonder if we have disqualified ourselves from the blessings mentioned in our patriarchal blessings or other priesthood blessings. Carefully read Doctrine and Covenants 3:6–11. Here is what verse 10 records: "But remember, God is merciful; therefore, repent of that which thou hast done which is contrary to the commandment which I gave you, and thou art still chosen, and art again called to the work."

Perhaps nowhere in scripture is the reality of Satan and his tactics spelled out more clearly than in Doctrine and Covenants section 10. The Lord is explaining to Joseph Smith what happened to the lost manuscript. Carefully read Doctrine and Covenants 10:6–29. Here is a partial list of Satan's tactics:

1. He caused men to alter the words Joseph had translated.
2. He stirs people up to do iniquity.
3. He stirs up people against the truths of the Restoration.
4. He deceives men into believing it is all right to lie to catch someone else in a lie.

You should also be aware what the Lord told Moses about Satan's tactics. In Moses 4:3–4, the Lord explains:

> Wherefore, because that Satan rebelled against me, and sought to destroy the agency of man, which I, the Lord God, had given him, and also, that I should give unto him mine own power; by the power of mine Only Begotten, I caused that he should be cast down;
>
> And he became Satan, yea, even the devil, the father of all lies, to deceive and to blind men, and to lead them captive at his will, even as many as would not hearken unto my voice.

Satan tries to destroy your agency. That happens every time we become addicted to any substance or activity that weakens our ability to choose for ourselves. He is the "father of all lies" and therefore he deceives us into believing we can break the commandments and not pay the penalty. He blinds us, making it nearly impossible to see clearly right from wrong. He leads captive those who will not follow the Lord and His prophets. In each of these tactics we can readily see friends or family members who are on that slippery slope leading to misery and self-destruction.

Over 2,400 years ago, Nephi saw our day and how Satan would deceive us. In 2 Nephi 28:19–22, Nephi records:

> For the kingdom of the devil must shake, and they which belong to it must needs be stirred up unto repentance, or the devil will grasp them with his everlasting chains, and they be stirred up to anger, and perish;
>
> For behold, at that day shall he rage in the hearts of the children of men, and stir them up to anger against that which is good.
>
> And others will he pacify, and lull them away into carnal security, that they will say: All is well in Zion; yea, Zion prospereth, all is well—and thus the devil cheateth their souls, and leadeth them away carefully down to hell.
>
> And behold, others he flattereth away, and telleth them there is no hell; and he saith unto them: I am no devil, for there is none—and thus he whispereth in their ears, until he grasps them with his awful chains, from whence there is no deliverance.

It seems like Satan is working both ends of the continuum. On the one hand, he is telling people there is no hell and he is no devil. How convenient. If people deny the existence of the devil and his angels, they can go undetected and uncontested, deceiving and destroying whomever they choose. You will be the voice testifying that Satan is real and warning people of his tactics. On the other hand, he lullabies us into believing that all is well and we don't need to worry about Satan because he isn't really an influence we have to cope with.

Nephi outlined how the devil and his angels would work among all people in the last days:

> And there are also secret combinations, even as in times of old, according to the combinations of the devil, for he is the founder of all these things; yea, the founder of murder, and works of darkness; yea, and he leadeth them by the neck with a flaxen cord, until he bindeth them with his strong cords forever. (2 Nephi 26:22)

Once again, be forewarned that you will be a primary target for the devil and his angels as you reveal him to your investigators and the world. The earlier you can detect his evil influence and take the steps to overcome the temptations, the more powerful you will be in helping others escape from his suffocating, soul-destroying grasp.

For your investigators:

You will undoubtedly come across people who will scoff at you for testifying that there is a devil. However, most of those people will also claim to be Christians. It is helpful to know what the Bible teaches about the devil since devote Christians will claim to believe every word in the Bible.

Here are a few references to the devil and his power from the Bible (emphasis added):

- Hebrews 2:14— ". . . that through death he might destroy *him that had the power of death*, that is, the devil."
- Revelation 12:9— ". . . that *old serpent*, called the Devil, and *Satan*, which deceiveth the whole world: he was cast out into the earth, and his angels were cast out with him."
- 1 Peter 5:8— "Be sober, be vigilant; because your adversary the devil, *as a roaring lion*, walketh about, seeking whom he may devour."
- Revelation 12:12— ". . . Woe to the inhabiters of the earth and of the sea! for the devil is come down unto you, having great wrath, *because he knoweth that he hath but a short time.*"
- 1 John 3:8— "*He that committeth sin* is of the devil; for the devil sinneth from the beginning."
- Mark 3:11— "And unclean spirits, when they saw him, fell down before him, and cried, saying, *Thou art the Son of God.*"
- Mark 1:34— "And he healed many that were sick of divers diseases, and cast out many devils; and *suffered not the devils to speak, because they knew him.*"

- Luke 4:41— "And devils also came out of many, crying out, and saying, *Thou art Christ the Son of God*. And he rebuking them suffered them not to speak: *for they knew that he was Christ*." (See also Matthew 8:28–29; Mark 5:2–7; Luke 8:28; James 2:19.)

There is no doubt that Christ knew that the devil and his angels were real spirit beings. Share your knowledge with those you teach but don't be discouraged if they give you that "Really?!" look.

Chapter 5

The Book of Mormon

From the very first communication after the First Vision, the Lord established the instrument to bring souls to Christ. On the Title Page of the Book of Mormon, the purpose for the book was stated: "To the convincing of the Jew and Gentile that Jesus is the Christ". That will be your challenge as a missionary.

Cement in your mind what the Lord, Himself, said about the Book of Mormon: "And he [Joseph Smith] has translated the book, even that part which I have commanded him, and as your Lord and your God liveth it is true" (D&C 17:6).

You may encounter people who will testify that God told them the Book of Mormon is false. Don't be distracted. The Lord's testimony trumps any alleged witness to the contrary.

What does the Book of Mormon contain that is so convincing and powerful? In Doctrine and Covenants 20:8–28 is an extensive list of some of the key doctrine from the Book of Mormon.

1. Book of Mormon is translated by the power of God. (verse 8)
2. It contains the fullness of the gospel. (verse 9)
3. Ministering of angels still happens. (verse 10)
4. It proves the scriptures are true and that God still calls men to the ministry. (verse 11)

5. God is the same yesterday, today, and forever. (verse 12)
6. The world will be judged by the Book of Mormon. (verse 13)
7. Faithful workers of righteousness will inherit eternal life. (verse 14)
8. Unbelief and rejection of Book of Mormon results in condemnation. (verse 15)
9. Book of Mormon proves there is a God in Heaven. (verse 17)
10. God created male and female in His own likeness. (verse 18)
11. God gave commandments to worship Him. (verse 19)
12. The Fall came by transgression of law. (verse 20)
13. God gave His Only Begotten to atone for all sins. (verse 21)
14. Christ suffered temptations but didn't give in. (verse 22)
15. Christ was crucified and then resurrected three days later. (verse 23)
16. Christ sits on the right hand of the Father. (verse 24)
17. Those who believe and are baptized will be saved. (verse 25)
18. Prophets spoke as moved upon by the Holy Ghost. (verse 26)
19. Holy Ghost bears witness of the Father and the Son. (verse 27)
20. Unity of the Godhead—one in purpose but separate in body and They are infinite and eternal. (verse 28)

In Doctrine and Covenants 1:29, the Savior testifies that the Book of Mormon was translated through the mercy and power of God. It was never claimed to be written by Joseph Smith. Carefully read sections 3, 5, and 10 to gain greater insights into why the Book of Mormon was written.

In Mormon 7:9, Mormon explains how the Book of Mormon is to be a second witness that the Bible is true. The Book of Mormon and the Bible testify of each other:

> For behold, this [Book of Mormon] is written for the intent that ye may believe that [Bible]; and if ye believe that [Bible] ye will believe this [Book of Mormon] also; and if ye believe this [Book of Mormon] ye will know concerning your fathers, and also the marvelous works which were wrought by the power of God among them.

Some people will try to say that the Book of Mormon contradicts the Bible on every page. Ask them for examples. I have never met anyone who made that claim who had ever read the Book of Mormon.

2 Nephi 29 is one of the powerful logical arguments against those who claim the Bible is total, complete, and will never allow for any more scripture. Read and mark that chapter carefully. Almost 2,500 years ago, the Lord told Nephi what men in our day would use to prevent people from seriously reading the Book of Mormon. One roadside billboard in Texas read: "Don't read the Book of Mormon and pray about it. That is how they get you!" What an admission that the Book of Mormon is fulfilling its designed purpose to bring souls to Christ.

For your investigators:

The Book of Mormon is the Lord's designated tool for conversion. No matter how smart you, the missionary, think you are or how persuasive your arguments are, nothing comes close to the power of the Book of Mormon in converting people and then holding them in the Church.

Make reading the Book of Mormon the challenge you issue from your very first meeting and every meeting thereafter. Testify from your own experience the truthfulness of Moroni's promise (Moroni 10:3–5) and how the Book of Mormon has changed your life.

If you fail to establish this foundation as part of their conversion, they will not stay active even if they are baptized out of love and respect for you as missionaries.

Citing favorite passages is good and helpful, but the Lord called Mormon to abridge a thousand years of history (being able to use only one one-hundredth of the material available to him) to weave a story that would develop faith in Christ and teach the gospel. The Nephites never had the Book of Mormon. It was written for our day. Over and over again (starting in 1 Nephi) Mormon shows how trusting in Christ, keeping His commandments, and enduring to the end resulted in prosperity and happiness. While breaking the commandments, forgetting God, and embracing the sins so common among mortals resulted in misery, death, and destruction.

We believe that reading the Book of Mormon from beginning to end is the most effective way of insuring true, lasting conversion.

Chapter 6

Call to Labor

More than a year before the Church was restored, many of the early brethren were anxious to share the rapidly unfolding knowledge with family and friends—indeed they wanted to share the gospel with the world.

The most famous section on missionary work was given to Joseph Smith's father, Joseph Smith Senior. In Doctrine and Covenants section 4, the Lord outlines the necessary motivation and qualifications to be a successful missionary. A quick summary may be helpful in cementing in your mind the starting place the Lord outlined for His future missionaries.

In verse 2 the Lord explains that He wants focused, fully engaged missionaries. You are to serve the Lord with *all* of your heart, might, mind, and strength. That is total involvement. There are three promised blessings for that focused service:

1. You will stand "blameless before God at the last days." (verse 2)
2. You will not perish—presumably at the destruction at the Second Coming or at the judgment day. (verse 4)
3. You will bring salvation to your soul. (verse 4)

To qualify to be on the Lord's first team in the last minutes of the fourth quarter of the super bowl of all time, you must have a burning "desire" (see verse 3). As essential as a self-generated desire is, that merely puts you in line to be considered. The qualifications for missionary service are listed in verse 5. They are:

1. Faith
2. Hope
3. Charity
4. Love
5. With an eye single to the glory of God

Remember God's work and His glory is to "bring to pass the immortality and eternal life of man" (see Moses 1:39)—that must be your singular focus.

But if you want to be a superstar on the Lord's first team, verse 6 adds more qualifications. You will note that two of those qualifiers listed above, faith and charity, are mentioned a second time, emphasizing the importance of these characteristics. The others not mentioned in the basic list of qualifications are:

1. Virtue
2. Knowledge
3. Temperance
4. Patience
5. Brotherly kindness
6. Godliness
7. Humility
8. Diligence

Then follows the first of many references to God's willingness to assist you in your efforts to share His gospel: "Ask, and ye shall receive; knock, and it shall be opened to you" (verse 7).

Hyrum Smith, the prophet's older brother, could hardly contain himself. He wanted to share the gospel "now" and not wait. In Doctrine and Covenants 11, the Lord had to slow him down and in so doing gave us some vital counsel to help us prepare. In verses 6, 9, 18, and 20, the Lord punctuated the absolute importance of *keeping His commandments*. You might think Hyrum must have been a wayward brother. On the contrary, Hyrum was one of the most faithful and obedient sons of our Heavenly Father. So why so much emphasis? In verse 27, the Lord generalizes this revelation to you and me and all who are called to serve. He says: "Behold, I speak unto all who have good desires, and have thrust in their sickle to reap."

The Lord continues His instructions in verse 9. He said His gospel is to be shared according to His commandments. Your mission president will be the one to set the directions for your mission. It may vary according to the geographical location where you are serving. Follow his counsel.

In verses 12–14, the Lord commands us to put our trust in His Spirit. You can tell when you are acting according to His Spirit because you will be led to:

1. Do good
2. Do justly
3. Walk humbly
4. Judge righteously

A wise preparing missionary will learn to live his or her life according to that Spirit long before entering the mission field.

What will that Spirit do for you—not only on your mission but throughout your life? The Lord says in verses 13 and 14 that He "will impart unto you of [His] Spirit which shall":

1. Enlighten your mind.
2. Fill your soul with joy.
3. Enable you to know anything you desire of Him.

From the testimonial of thousands of college students in my classes, they testified that they could learn ten times the amount of knowledge in one-tenth the time when the Spirit was with them.

Then the Lord cautions Hyrum (and by extension all of us): You "need not suppose that you are called to preach until you are called" (verse 15). So, what are we to do in the meantime? Verses 21 and 22 give His answer (emphasis added):

> Seek not to declare my word, but first seek to obtain my word, and then shall your tongue be loosed; then, if you desire, you shall have my Spirit and my word, yea, the power of God unto the convincing of men.
>
> But now hold your peace; *study my word which hath gone forth* among the children of men, and also *study my word which shall come forth* among the children of men, or that which is now translating, yea, until you have obtained all which I shall grant unto the children of men in this generation, and then shall all things be added thereto.

There you have the Lord's sequence for preparing: Study the scriptures that have been printed. Study also the counsel given through His living prophets. You have plenty to do to prepare. Everything you do now to prepare will make you that much more powerful when you enter the mission field after "being called."

Some of you may have a high paying job, or a special someone who wants you to stay home and get married, or you have a scholarship—any number of reasons I have heard over forty years of teaching. However, the Lord (who knows everything) stated and then emphasized what was the most valuable thing you could do.

To two young Whitmer brothers (John and Peter Jr.) when they asked Joseph what was most important and productive, the Lord said:

> For many times you have desired of me to know that which would be of the most worth unto you. . . . And now, behold, I say unto you that the thing which will be of the most worth unto you will be to declare repentance unto this people, that you may bring souls unto me, that you may rest with them in the kingdom of my Father. (D&C 15:4, 6; 16:4, 6)

No matter what you or I may think, the All-Knowing God has spelled out the answer in unmistakable words what is the most valuable way we can spend our time before beginning our adult life.

Several years later, the Lord answered those who want to decide for themselves when they should serve.

> Hearken, O ye who have given your names to go forth to proclaim my gospel, and to prune my vineyard.
>
> Behold, I say unto you that it is my will that you should go forth and not tarry, neither be idle but labor with your might. (D&C 75:2–3)

The gospel is being spread so rapidly throughout the world that the Lord has made multiple opportunities to serve if a full-time proselyting mission is not a possibility for you. Please contact your bishop and stake president for alternate mission opportunities. They are just as valuable and necessary as proselyting mission are.

Perhaps it would be well to take a minute and elaborate a little on the rewards for service. Although "what's in it for me" is not the reason we serve, you might be interested in what the Lord said faithful missionaries would receive.

Although the blessings for faithful service are scattered through the four standard works, Mark 10:28–30 gives a very good, concise explanation. Just a little background. A rich young man had come to the Savior asking what he needed to do to qualify for eternal life. The Savior told him to "keep the commandments" and then He listed six of the original Ten Commandments. Evidently the young man was (in our way of speaking today) an Eagle Scout, a seminary graduate, assistant to the Bishop in the Priest's quorum, daily read the scriptures, and kept all of the commandments Church leaders had given him.

Mark then records:

> Then Jesus beholding him loved him, and said unto him, One thing thou lackest: go thy way, sell whatsoever thou hast, and give to the poor, and thou shalt have treasure in heaven: and come, take up the cross, and follow me [in other words: come on a mission!].
>
> And he was sad at that saying, and went away grieved: for he had great possessions. (Mark 10:21–22)

At that point the Savior gives the thought-provoking statement about a camel going through the eye of a needle being easier than a rich man, who trusts in riches, to enter into the celestial kingdom.

Peter, who generally asks the questions we want the answer to, says: "Lo, we have left all, and have followed thee." As if to say: "we have given up everything and followed You. What is in it for us?" Mark continues:

> And Jesus answered and said, Verily I say unto you, There is no man that hath left house, or brethren, or sisters, or father, or mother, or wife, or children, or lands, for my sake, and the gospel's,
>
> But he shall receive an hundredfold now in this time, houses, and brethren, and sisters, and mothers, and children, and lands, with persecutions; and in the world to come eternal life. (Mark 10:28–30)

Note the Savior's promised blessings:

1. A hundred times the blessings of houses and barns (i.e. physical possessions)
2. A hundred times brethren, mothers, children. Not that you would have a hundred wives or a hundred children—that may not be a blessing here on earth! But the quality of your relationship would be one hundred times better if you use what you will learn while on your mission.
3. Eternal life in the world to come. Eternal life is the highest degree of the celestial kingdom. Not a bad exchange for eighteen or twenty-four months in His service!

Your selfless service has not only personal promised blessings but extends to blessing your family as well. The Lord said:

> Therefore, thrust in your sickle with all your soul, and your sins are forgiven you, and you shall be laden with sheaves upon your back, for the laborer is worthy of his hire. Wherefore, your family shall live. (D&C 31:5)

If you are still wondering whether some kind of mission is a personal choice, perhaps a careful reading of Doctrine and Covenants 36:4–7 can clarify the answer to that question (emphasis added):

> And now this calling and commandment give I unto you concerning *all men*—
>
> That as many as shall come before my servants Sidney Rigdon and Joseph Smith, Jun., embracing this calling and commandment, shall be ordained and sent forth to preach the everlasting gospel among the nations—
>
> Crying repentance, saying: Save yourselves from this untoward generation, and come forth out of the fire, hating even the garments spotted with the flesh.
>
> And *this commandment shall be given unto the elders of my church*, that every man which will embrace it with singleness of heart may be ordained and sent forth, even as I have spoken.

Of course, our names are not presented before Joseph Smith and Sidney Rigdon but you receive your call from the President of the Church who stands in the same position that Joseph Smith did.

Joseph Smith taught:

> Every man who has a calling to minister to the inhabitants of the world was ordained to that very purpose in the Grand Council of heaven before this world was. I suppose that I was ordained to this very office in that Grand Council. *(History of the Church*, 6:364)

What a privilege! What an opportunity! What a responsibility! No wonder the Lord told Thomas B. Marsh: "Lift up your heart and rejoice, for the hour of your mission is come; and your tongue shall be loosed, and you shall declare glad tidings of great joy unto this generation" (D&C 31:3).

Just showing up to the MTC with little or no preparation, will result in a lot of wasted time as you try to catch up. Avoid that disappointment and frustration by preparing more diligently right now!

For your Investigators:

Perhaps, other than planting the seeds of a mission in the heart and mind of a young man or young woman you are teaching, this chapter is focused specifically for you—the preparing missionary.

Chapter 7

Answers to Prayers

It is no coincidence that the Lord places a discussion on receiving answers to prayers immediately following the call to labor. The Lord never intended that the witness to the truthfulness of His gospel should come by physical proofs. He did not delegate the granting of testimony to angels, to what others may say, or the internet, or anything or anyone else. He promised to bear witness to the truthfulness of the gospel through a member of the Godhead—the Holy Ghost.

It would be difficult to overstate the importance of you gaining a personal testimony that God really does answer prayers. Oliver Cowdery's experience, when he wanted a confirmation that the translation of the Book of Mormon really was God's will, provides a good place to start in understanding how to recognize an answer to prayer.

Oliver had already had a vision about Joseph having the plates while he was staying with the Smith's in Palmyra, New York. He decided to travel to Pennsylvania to meet Joseph Smith. Oliver arrived in Harmony, Pennsylvania on April 5, 1829. He started acting as a scribe for Joseph Smith two days later. On that very day, he asked for a re-confirmation. The Lord revealed:

> Verily, verily, I say unto thee, blessed art thou for what thou hast done; for thou hast inquired of me, and behold, as often as thou hast inquired thou hast received instruction

> of my Spirit. If it had not been so, thou wouldst not have come to the place where thou art at this time. (D&C 6:14)

Two things are of special note in this verse:

1. "As often as thou hast inquired"—in other words, God answers every sincere prayer.
2. Answers to prayers always motivate us to action. The more you expect to get an answer, the more you will be watchful to recognize the answer. Then you must be prepared to act on the impressions that you get.

The Lord continues: "Behold, thou knowest that thou hast inquired of me and I did enlighten thy mind; and now I tell thee these things that thou mayest know that thou hast been enlightened by the Spirit of truth" (D&C 6:15).

The third part of recognizing answers to prayer is to note carefully what thoughts are flooding into your mind. The Lord tells Oliver that He is explaining this part of how prayers are answered specifically so he will recognize when he is receiving answers.

Oliver was pretty sure at that time that he understood all about answers to prayers. The Lord, however, had much more to reveal. In verse 22, the Lord reminds Oliver of a night in Palmyra, New York at the home of Joseph Smith Sr. when he prayed to find out whether Joseph really had the plates after hearing about it from the Smith family. The Lord then says: "Did I not speak peace to your mind concerning the matter? What greater witness can you have than from God?" (D&C 6:23)

You will discover that the working of the Spirit brings peace—even in times of turmoil. In fact, the ancient apostle Paul, told the saints in Philippi: "And the peace of God, which passeth all understanding, shall keep your hearts and minds through Christ Jesus" (Philippians 4:7).

Oliver was pretty sure he would never question again, but two sections later he is again questioning. Oliver was not only a schoolteacher but also a lawyer so he reasoned that he was accustomed to manipulating his mind to believe whatever he wanted to believe. The Lord used

Oliver's questioning to continue educating us on how to recognize answer to prayers.

In Doctrine and Covenants 8:2–3, the Lord said:

> Yea, behold, I will tell you in your mind and in your heart, by the Holy Ghost, which shall come upon you and which shall dwell in your heart.
>
> Now, behold, this is the spirit of revelation; behold, this is the spirit by which Moses brought the children of Israel through the Red Sea on dry ground.

The Lord had already addressed that answers will come to the mind. Now He adds the other domain: *the heart*. But note carefully, the Lord did not say He would answer in the mind *or* the heart. He said *answers would come in both the mind AND the heart*. Why that emphasis? Because either you or the adversary can manipulate one domain or the other, but neither you nor the adversary can manipulate both domains at the same time or it would negate the "spirit of revelation."

As an example, the Lord used a very familiar Old Testament story to illustrate His point. We may have become accustomed to thinking Moses knew exactly what to do when his progress in leading the Children of Israel out of Egypt was blocked by the Red Sea and he received the report that Pharaoh and his armies were closing in on the rear.

For the sake of illustration, could we propose a hypothetical conversation between the Lord and Moses at that life and death situation?

Moses: Lord, you've got a serious problem. The Red Sea blocks our way and the armies of Pharaoh are behind.

The Lord: No, Moses, *you* have a problem. You're down there. I'm up here. What do you want me to do about it?

Moses: Hold off Pharaoh's armies while I figure this out.

The Lord puts a pillar of fire between the Children of Israel and the oncoming army. *[Just as a note of interest: it was a pillar of light and fire to the Children of Israel but a cloud of darkness to Pharaoh's armies (see Exodus 14:20).]*

Now Moses begins to try to solve the problem of the Red Sea.

Moses: Okay, Lord, You hold off the armies of Pharaoh and we'll march around the Red Sea. When we get to the other side, turn them loose and we'll wave them farewell as we march off to the Promised Land.

The Lord: Good plan, Moses. Cast thine eyes to the left and the right.

Doing so, Moses saw that the Red Sea is huge—not something to walk around in a day or two. *[Back to the drawing board.]*

Moses: Okay, I have another idea. We'll cut down trees and make rafts and when we get beyond the reach of their arrows, turn them loose and we'll thumb our noses at them as we sail off to the Promised Land.

The Lord: Good idea, Moses. Which tree do you want to start with?

There are no trees lining the Red Sea!

Moses, frustrated: Well, why don't we just part the sea and walk through!

How did the Lord signify that Moses had hit upon the right solution? He (the Lord) told him in his mind *and* his heart.

Although that is a fictitious dialogue between the Lord and His prophet, it demonstrates the next point. In order to continue Oliver's schooling on how to get an answer to prayer, the Lord gives Oliver the opportunity to translate from the golden plates. Oliver was very excited and gave it a try, translating only a few words. You may think that he didn't translate but Doctrine and Covenants 9:5 contains the explanation on why he failed—he didn't continue as he commenced. Now for the lesson that can benefit you and your investigators for the rest of your lives.

In verse 7, the Lord says: "Behold, you have not understood; you have supposed that I would give it unto you, when you took no thought save it was to ask me." Too often people want the Lord to make all their decisions for them. The Lord already knows everything, we are here to learn how to become like Him. Here is a little couplet that seems to state an eternal principle: "Whoever must eventually stand judgment for the decision must be free to make the decision."

Having taught thousands of young single adults at BYU–Provo, marriage was the most pressing topic on their minds. Often, they wanted the Lord to tell them who to marry. Since the Lord was not going to be the one to live with their spouse, it seems reasonable that they should make the decision and then ask for confirmation—which is exactly what the Lord instructs next.

In verse 8 the Lord explains:

> But, behold, I say unto you, that you must study it [whatever problem you are facing] out in your mind; then you must ask me if it [the decision you have arrived at by weighing all the pro's and con's] be right, and if it [the unwavering decision you have arrived at] is right I will cause that your bosom shall burn within you; therefore, you shall feel that it is right.

Why not: "You will *know* it is right?" Because by your own intellectual research and analysis you have already come to the conclusion that you "know" is right. Now the Lord is adding the other dimension—the heart!

What if either you or the adversary has come up with the wrong decision? The Lord addressed that in verse 9:

> But if it [the decision you made] be not right you shall have no such feelings, but you shall have a stupor of thought that shall cause you to forget [or as Melvin J. Ballard put it: "Shall turn your heart away from"] the thing which is wrong; therefore, you cannot write that which is sacred save it be given you from me. (See Melvin J. Ballard, Conference Report, April 1931, 37–38.)

I want to use a personal story to cement this very important principle. A number of years ago I served as bishop of a singles ward at BYU. One day a twenty-seven-year-old, single young man came to my office to renew his temple recommend. As he sat down, I had a thought flash across my mind and asked, "Are you any closer to marriage today than you were six years ago when you returned from your mission?"

He grimaced and said, "Gee, Bishop, I wish you had asked me that question yesterday."

"Why?"

"I just broke my fourth engagement yesterday."

"Don't you love the girl?"

"I worship the ground on which she walks."

"Then why don't you marry her?"

"The Lord told me she is the wrong one!"

"How do you know the Lord told you she was the wrong one?"

"It is always the same. We get engaged, have our pictures taken for the wedding announcements [and then he added "I don't know why the Lord waits until after the pictures are taken. It is awfully expensive!"], and then it happened again."

Becoming somewhat frustrated, I asked, "What happened again?"

"When I got home yesterday, I was sitting in my apartment pondering about being married to the girl of my dreams and I had a sudden wave of doubt and fear come over me and I knew the Lord was telling me this was not the right one!"

"You jerk! Don't you know that God never uses doubt and fear as a negative answer?"

"Run that by me one more time, Bishop."

"God never uses doubt and fear as a negative answer."

Then I quoted the following three scriptures: "For God hath not given us the spirit of fear; but of power, and of love, and of a sound mind" (2 Timothy 1:7). If "fear" doesn't come from God, where does it come from? If you answer, "from the devil," you are correct. Why would we listen to him? His stated objective is to "make us miserable like unto himself" (see 2 Nephi 2:18, 27). How is he (the devil) miserable? He is single, he is the father of lies, and will eventually be cast out forever from the presence of God. Everything that has Satan's fingerprints on it will lead us in that direction.

Second scripture: "Ye endeavored to believe that ye should receive the blessing which was offered unto you; but behold, verily I say unto you there were fears in your hearts, and verily this is the reason that ye did not receive" (D&C 67:3). He asked, "You mean, fear blocks answers to prayers?" It certainly does according to what the Lord has revealed.

Then one final scripture. "Look unto me in every thought; doubt not, fear not" (D&C 6:36). In one short verse the Lord informs us that He doesn't use doubt or fear as a negative answer.

As I looked at him, he seemed rather uncomfortable. He asked if we could postpone the recommend interview until the next day, to which I agreed. The following day I heard a knock on my door and I invited whoever was there to come in. My ward member opened the door and stuck his head in with a big smile on his face. Rather insensitively, I asked, "Oh, did you find number five?" To which he laughingly replied, "No, but I did find number four!" He asked if his fiancé could come in with him and chat for a minute. I responded in the positive. A beautiful young lady came in sporting an engagement ring. He said, "Bishop, how did you know that I didn't receive a negative answer?" I said, "Because you had what you considered to be a 'stupor of thought' but your heart was not turned away from her."

If it had been a true negative response from the Lord, the logic he had used to determine she was the right one would have broken down and his desire to be with her would have evaporated. Then I reminded him that either he or the adversary could duplicate one domain (heart or mind) but neither he nor the adversary could duplicate them both at the same time or that would negate the spirit of revelation.

For your investigators:

Unless they understand the difference between Satan attempting to answer their prayers and the Lord's explained formula, some may say they prayed and God told them the Church was not true or Joseph Smith was not a prophet, or the Book of Mormon was false. Please be assured that they are not getting their answer from the right source. The Lord bears His testimony about the truthfulness of the Church in Doctrine and Covenants 1:30, of the Book of Mormon in Doctrine and Covenants 17:6, and of Joseph Smith in Doctrine and Covenants 20:2 and multiple other places.

The power of your testimony will be based upon your personal experience with the answer to prayers. Take what time is necessary to get that rock-solid testimony so that when you bear it to your investigators, the Lord can confirm by the Holy Ghost that what you are bearing testimony of is true.

Chapter 8

Priesthood Power, Church Organization

There are many churches on the earth. What makes our church different from all the others? There are any number of things, but the first is priesthood. What is the priesthood that separates us from all others? When Jesus was preparing His apostles to spread the gospel, He first called them together and "he gave them power" (Matthew 10:1). Although there are many definitions of priesthood, possibly the best is the shortest: "The Power of God."

That same power the Savior bestowed upon His original Apostles was bestowed upon Joseph Smith and Oliver Cowdery. First, the Aaronic Priesthood was restored by John the Baptist (see D&C 13). Next, the Melchizedek Priesthood was restored by Peter, James, and John.

Before young men depart for the mission field, they are ordained to the higher or Melchizedek Priesthood. Both elders and sisters are set apart by their stake president as he exercises the priesthood keys, authority, and power in his office.

Young men are given a six-year training period with a number of assigned duties all designed to prepare them for the Melchizedek Priesthood. Unfortunately, too many young men fail to learn their duties and magnify their offices in the Aaronic Priesthood. That is the same as having the keys to a sports car and never putting the key in the ignition switch.

When hands are laid on a young man's head, he is given the authority, or priesthood. However, the power doesn't come automatically. He must keep the commandments and magnify his office. Then he will sense the power he was given access to when he was ordained.

Open your Doctrine and Covenants and carefully read section 20 verses 38–60. These verses will outline the Lord's expectations for elders, priests, teachers, and deacons. Whether others in your quorum are fulfilling their duties or not, isn't the point. If you want to be a powerful missionary, you must prepare by doing what the Lord requires.

Although priesthood is mentioned in many of the sections of the Doctrine and Covenants, five sections are devoted almost exclusively to broadening our understanding of it. It would be well if you read all of them: 13, 20, 84, 107, and 121.

As you magnify your calling, be particularly aware of how you feel. You will literally feel God's power growing inside you. The more diligent you are in magnifying your calling, the more satanic opposition you will experience. Rather than make the mistake of thinking you are bad because of the endless temptations, see them as what they really are—Satan's attempts to destroy you before you get the Melchizedek Priesthood, which, along with many other things, is the power to cast him out. With the additional temptations from the adversary comes the additional strength through the priesthood to overcome the temptations.

Many young men won't begin to take the priesthood seriously until they are about to be ordained elders. The Melchizedek Priesthood has more power than the Aaronic Priesthood but also more responsibilities. In Doctrine and Covenants 84:33–44 the Lord reveals the "Oath and Covenant" of the priesthood. It is well worth our time to take a serious look at what the Lord says and make sure we are willing to accept the responsibilities which come with the priesthood.

If you are faithful in obtaining the two priesthoods (Aaronic and Melchizedek) *and* magnifying your calling—magnifying not only implies enlarging but also focusing on our particular calling like the rays of the sun are not increased by a magnifying glass but are focused on a certain point—there are a number of blessings which follow:

- You are sanctified by the Spirit unto the renewing of your body. You don't hear of men putting their hands on their own heads and giving themselves a blessing. It is in blessing others that you are sanctified (i.e. made holy) and renewed.
- You become the "sons of Moses"—he was a prophet. You would have power to prophesy for those over whom you have stewardship. Don't try to prophesy for the world—that is the assigned task of the First Presidency and the Quorum of the Twelve Apostles.
- You become the "sons of Aaron"—he was a priest. As such you have the responsibility to care for the temporal or physical needs of those you have stewardship over.
- You become the "seed of Abraham"—he was a patriarch. You have the right to give blessings to your wife and children as much as the stake patriarch does. You must receive inspiration or revelation as the stake patriarch does in order to know what blessings to pronounce.
- You become the "church and kingdom and elect of God" (verse 34).

Although all of these blessings can and do refer to conditions on earth, they are also used as descriptions of those in the celestial kingdom. The Lord doesn't expect that you will automatically know how to use His priesthood, so He promises: "And also all they who receive this priesthood receive me, saith the Lord" (verse 35). He will prompt, inspire, direct, and guide you on the proper use of His priesthood.

Additional helps come as the Lord says: "For he that receiveth my servants receiveth me" (verse 36). Quorum leaders, bishoprics, stake presidencies, and General Authorities all give counsel and set the example on how to magnify your priesthood. Follow them!

Then the Savior gives the greatest of all promises: "And he that receiveth me receiveth my Father" (verse 37). With the acceptance of the Father and the Son comes the promised blessing:

> And he that receiveth my Father receiveth my Father's kingdom; therefore all that my Father hath shall be given unto him.
>
> And this is according to the oath and covenant which belongeth to the priesthood.
>
> Therefore, all those who receive the priesthood, receive this oath and covenant of my Father, which he cannot break, neither can it be moved. (D&C 84:38–40)

It is hard to comprehend the promised blessings for faithfully magnifying the priesthood. However, there is a stern warning associated with getting the priesthood and doing nothing with it. In verse 41, the Lord says: "But whoso breaketh this covenant after he hath received it, and altogether turneth therefrom, shall not have forgiveness of sins in this world nor in the world to come."

Consider seriously before you are ordained to the Melchizedek priesthood and promise yourself that you will be faithful for the rest of your life. Some may say, "I'm not sure I want to get the priesthood. The responsibilities are too great!" However, in verse 42, the Lord states: "And wo unto all those who come not unto this priesthood." There has been much said about being foreordained to be a bearer of the priesthood (see Alma 13:1–6).

Now a couple of verses which we often overlook. In verse 43, the Lord states (emphasis added): "And I now give unto you a commandment to *beware concerning yourselves,* to give diligent heed to the words of eternal life." What makes this verse sobering? Up until now you have had parents, teachers, quorum leaders, and bishops to tell you what to do and guide your footsteps. The Lord is saying that with the ordination to the Melchizedek Priesthood you ought to take responsibility for your own actions. If a movie is violent or pornographic, no one needs to tell you to leave—you must stand for what you know is right. If you are at a party and things are shaping up to drink something you know is wrong or engage in activities you know violate the moral code, you must develop the strength to get up and leave. As you read the scriptures, listen to the living prophets, and give heed to the promptings of the Spirit within you, you will see your progress towards perfection happening faster than you ever imagined.

Then in verse 44, the Lord says: "For you [the Melchizedek Priesthood bearer] shall live by every word that proceedeth forth from the mouth of God." Remember in Doctrine and Covenants 1:38: "Whether by my own voice or the voice of my servants—it is the same."

As you read the Doctrine and Covenants, you will see the Lord put the different offices in the Church. In section 20:2–3, the Lord names Joseph Smith and Oliver Cowdery as apostles and the first and second elders of the Church. Later in that section (as noted above), the Lord names elders, priests, teachers, and deacons. In verses 66 and 67, the Lord names bishops and high councilors. Throughout the Doctrine and Covenants, you will note when the Lord responds to the growing Church membership by organizing the First Presidency, the Quorum of the Twelve, and the Quorums of the Seventy.

You may wonder why other churches cannot function up to the celestial standard without the Melchizedek Priesthood. The Lord answers that question:

> And this greater priesthood administereth the gospel and holdeth the key of the mysteries of the kingdom, even the key of the knowledge of God.
>
> Therefore, in the ordinances thereof, the power of godliness is manifest.
>
> And without the ordinances thereof, and the authority of the priesthood, the power of godliness is not manifest unto men in the flesh;
>
> For without this no man can see the face of God, even the Father, and live. (D&C 84:19–22)

For now, the most important thing to understand is that the Lord Himself organized the Church and put officers in those callings. Many times, as a missionary you will meet people who say, "I'm spiritual but I'm not religious." Meaning that they are trying to establish their own way back to God. Make sure you understand that the ordinances necessary for salvation and exaltation are housed only within the Church.

For your investigators:

There are many Bible scriptures pointing to the priesthood and Church organization. As you read the New Testament, it will become evident that it is the Lord who calls and ordains people to callings—not something that they take upon themselves. "And no man taketh this honour unto himself, but he that is called of God, as was Aaron" (Hebrews 5:4).

The Lord said: "Ye have not chosen me, but I have chosen you, and ordained you, that ye should go and bring forth fruit, and that your fruit should remain: that whatsoever ye shall ask of the Father in my name, he may give it you" (John 15:16).

Many churches deny the necessity of having priesthood. Many other churches will claim their authority from the Bible or some theological college. Others feel that a mere desire to be a preacher is sufficient to empower them.

You may discuss with them (but don't argue!) what Paul taught about the role of apostles and prophets in Christ's church (see Ephesians 2:19–20). Then follow up that discussion by reading Ephesians 4:11–14. Paul gives the purpose for the offices—perfecting the saints, the work of the ministry, and edifying the body of Christ—which is the Church.

How long did Paul say they would be necessary? "Till we all come to a unity of the faith" (verse 13). The fact that there are hundreds of Christian churches, each with somewhat varying doctrine, ought to testify that we are not at a unity of the faith—hence we need apostles and prophets.

Especially in today's world, where people seem to think they can change God's commandments either by legislation or just disregarding them, it would be well to review with your investigators what Paul told the Galatians:

> I marvel that ye are so soon removed from him that called you into the grace of Christ unto another gospel:
>
> Which is not another; but there be some that trouble you, and would pervert the gospel of Christ.

> But though we, or an angel from heaven, preach any other gospel unto you than that which we have preached unto you, let him be accursed.
>
> As we said before, so say I now again, If any man preach any other gospel unto you than that ye have received, let him be accursed. (Galatians 1:6–9)

Remember, this is not "Mormon Doctrine"—this comes from the very Bible that all Christians accept as the revealed will of God.

Since you represent the only Church on the face of the earth that is organized as Christ organized His Church, you are bound to face some Christians who want to argue that apostles and prophets are no longer necessary. You are not sent forth to "convert" people to the gospel—that is the role of the Holy Ghost. You are the messenger. Present your message by the power of the Spirit. According to Doctrine and Covenants 100:5–8, the Lord promises that He will send forth the Spirit to testify of the truths you have taught. If the Spirit is there, they will understand, rejoice, and be edified by what you are saying (see D&C 50:22). Then they must exercise their agency to accept or reject the message.

Chapter 9

The Worth of Souls

Although you may have been taught all of your life the Primary song "I Am a Child of God," it requires a deeper study to see all mankind as spirit offspring of God. That understanding comes from your understanding of the pre-earth life. "The Family—A Proclamation to the World" (something you ought to carry with you throughout your mission and your life) states:

> All human beings—male and female—are created in the image of God. Each is a beloved spirit son daughter of heavenly parents, and, as such, each has a divine nature and destiny. Gender is an essential characteristic of individual premortal, mortal, and eternal identity and purpose.

You will undoubtedly meet people on your mission and throughout your life who differ greatly from your active Latter-day Saint family and friends. Some are living life the best they know how, and it is easy to envision them as Latter-day Saints. However, a growing majority seem to be struggling to find a purpose in life or have chosen lifestyles that are opposite from what you know to be true.

The challenge for you is to look beyond the surface and see the potential of each human being. Almost a year before the Church was restored, the Lord revealed the worth of each individual on earth.

"Remember the worth of souls is great in the sight of God" (D&C 18:10).

In order to punctuate how much a soul is worth, you might ponder the following fantasy. Some evil power has taken God hostage and claims to have the power to destroy Him unless you pay a ransom. How much would you be willing to pay to save God if you had all the wealth of the universe? Likely you would say, "I'd pay anything to rescue God." Now consider what is the divine potential of every person on earth? What are you willing to give to ransom them from Satan's power? What does God say He was willing to give to ransom mankind?

> For, behold, the Lord your Redeemer suffered death in the flesh; wherefore he suffered the pain of all men, that all men might repent and come unto him.
>
> And he hath risen again from the dead, that he might bring all men unto him, on conditions of repentance. (D&C 18:11–12)

God was willing to sacrifice His sinless, Only Begotten Son, to ransom us from death and hell. Did He consider the sacrifice a good trade? "And how great is his joy in the soul that repenteth!" (D&C 18:13)

How did God set up the ransoming of His spirit children? "Wherefore, you are called to cry repentance unto this people" (verse 14). Participating with God in the ransoming of His spirit children comes with the following (well known) promise:

> And if it so be that you should labor all your days in crying repentance unto this people, and bring, save it be one soul unto me, how great shall be your joy with him in the kingdom of my Father!
>
> And now, if your joy will be great with one soul that you have brought unto me into the kingdom of my Father, how great will be your joy if you should bring many souls unto me!" (D&C 18:15–16)

Since we have been fantasizing the worth of souls, let's continue a possible future scene. Now millions of years have passed since you lived on earth. You and your eternal companion are now surveying the millions of worlds and billions of your spirit children as they are working through their mortal existence. You get a call on your cell phone ("celestial phone"). The voice on the other end asks if you have a minute to talk. Since time is no longer an issue, you agree. In an instant, a beautiful, glorified, exalted couple are kneeling before you and kissing your feet. You raise them up. As you look at them, you remember the young couple you helped bring into the Church while you were serving your mission. With tears streaming down their faces, they thank you for sharing the gospel with them.

You recall that you thought your mission was a failure because you only helped this one couple join the Church. However, with a sweep of his hand, your convert opens to your vision millions of worlds peopled by billions of their spirit children. Then turning to you, he says, "All of these owe their existence to you. Thank you for not giving up on us!" Your joy is complete and beyond human words to describe.

Is that an impossible dream? Not according to the above verses. Could I share one personal experience? While serving as a mission president, I was required to interview any candidate for baptism who'd had an abortion (there were several other reasons also). One evening, the missionaries had scheduled a "second interview" (that is what they call the mission president's interview) with a woman who had been a prostitute. They had taught her and now she wanted to be baptized but, because of her profession, she'd had several abortions.

Sister Bott waited with the missionaries in the foyer as I interviewed the woman in the stake president's office. After telling her story, accompanied with many tears, I told her I would bow my head and ask Heavenly Father for His approval for her to be baptized. She was so sure that the Lord wouldn't accept her, given her very rough past.

The answer was immediate, unmistakable, and powerful. The Lord gave His approval. As I told her of the manifestation I had just received, she was so thrilled that she reached across the desk separating us and put her arms around me as she wept and expressed her appreciation. The thought crossed my mind, "I'm being embraced by a prostitute!" I then received the sternest rebuke I have ever had. It was non-verbal but very distinct: "Dear President Bott. This is one of my choice and chosen daughters who got started off on the wrong foot. The blood of My Son will make her as clean as the day she was born!"

With that I put my arms around her and we wept together—she, because of Heavenly Father's love in allowing the Atonement to cleanse her, and me, because I gained a testimony of the worth of souls that has never left me.

If you could learn, as young as you are, to see people through the eyes of God, you would be positioning yourself as a powerful, Christ-like missionary. Start today looking at *everybody* as a potential god or goddess.

Until you can look beyond the outside, and see into the peoples' hearts, you will never be a powerful missionary. Many people you will encounter will have had a very difficult past or are living in less than ideal conditions. If you can envision them standing in white, ready to enter the temple, you will approach them in a more Christ-like way. Don't let the smell of tobacco smoke or the stench of alcohol deter you from sharing with them your vision of who they really are.

For your Investigators:

Many of the people you will meet will have been so beaten down that they have no vision or hope of the future. Since "wickedness never was happiness" (Alma 41:10), they may have resigned themselves to finding happiness or pleasure by escaping the pain of their living conditions. You are there to give them the vision of who they are and what they can become.

Don't you try to make the judgment whether they are prepared to hear the gospel—that is up to them. Your role is to present the truth to them in such a way that they cannot misunderstand. The Spirit will help you know what to say, how much to teach, and who is ready for the restored gospel.

Chapter 10

Who to Preach to?

This may sound like a dumb question—who to preach to? You may be inclined to say, "Everyone!" But that is not what the Lord teaches us: "And ye are called to bring to pass the gathering of mine elect; *for mine elect hear my voice and harden not their hearts*" (D&C 29:7, emphasis added).

If you will take note and not try to pursue your own thoughts, you can minimize the time you waste on people who are not yet ready to hear and accept the gospel. That doesn't mean that they won't ever be ready but, just as picking an apple before it is ripe leaves a bitter taste in your mouth, so trying to force a person to accept the gospel before they are ready will result in an equally negative experience.

The Lord informed us that there are *many* people who are ready to join the Church. Your job is to find them.

> For there are many yet on the earth among all sects, parties, and denominations, who are blinded by the subtle craftiness of men, whereby they lie in wait to deceive, and who are only kept from the truth because they know not where to find it. (D&C 123:12)

These good people are not all concentrated in one place. There are people prepared to receive the gospel from you no matter where you are called. Again, the Lord said:

> Wherefore, go ye and preach my gospel, whether to the north or to the south, to the east or to the west, it mattereth not, for ye cannot go amiss.
>
> Therefore, declare the things which ye have heard, and verily believe, and know to be true.
>
> Behold, this is the will of him who hath called you, your Redeemer, even Jesus Christ. (D&C 80:3–5)

It is true that some areas of the world seem more ready to accept the gospel, but the Lord said:

> Behold, the field is white already to harvest; therefore, whoso desireth to reap, let him thrust in his sickle with his might, and reap while the day lasts, that he may treasure up for his soul everlasting salvation in the kingdom of God. (D&C 6:3)

We know, however, that the great polarization of humanity is under way. Those who are ready to accept the gospel are to be "harvested" while those who reject the gospel are positioning themselves to be "burned." Note this language which certifies the separation:

> You shall begin to preach from this time forth, yea, to reap in the field which is white already to be burned. (D&C 31:4)

The Lord told you how to recognize those who are ready to be taught. He said they would not harden their hearts but would hear His voice. Remember again: "By mine own voice or the voice of my servants, it is the same" (D&C 1:38). So your voice becomes His voice.

Even before you have a chance to speak with people, the Lord has given yet another method of determining where you will have the most success.

> And *there are none that doeth good except those who are ready to receive the fulness of my gospel*, which I have sent forth unto this generation. (D&C 35:12, emphasis added)

As you mingle among the people in your area, look for those who are doing good, who are serving others, or who lend a helping hand when there is work to be done. Sometimes inviting non-members to help with a Church clean-up or town clean-up projects will enable you to quickly identify those who, like Christ, "went about doing good" (see Acts 10:38).

Far too often, missionaries have the mistaken idea that they must be smart enough to answer any question (though there is nothing wrong with knowing the answer to difficult questions), or to be inviting enough to cause people to love them (though there is nothing wrong with people loving the missionaries), but you must remember you are merely the messenger to bring them to Christ.

If the people join the Church because of the missionaries, they will leave as soon as the missionaries are transferred. Having been a young missionary years ago in Samoa, twice a stake mission president (an office no longer used in the Church), a mission president, and a senior missionary in Hawaii and in Australia, I have wondered why the Lord chose young, basically uneducated, sometimes immature boys and girls to be the first (and sometimes the only) contact that people have to the gospel. He answers both of these questions:

> That the fulness of my gospel might be proclaimed by *the weak and the simple* unto the ends of the world, and before kings and rulers. (D&C 1:23, emphasis added)

> Wherefore, I call upon the *weak* things of the world, those who are *unlearned and despised,* to thresh the nations by the power of my Spirit;

> And their arm shall be my arm, and I will be their shield and their buckler; and I will gird up their loins, and they shall fight manfully for me; and their enemies shall be under their feet; and I will let fall the sword in their behalf, and by the fire of mine indignation will I preserve them.

> And the poor and the meek shall have the gospel preached unto them, and they shall be looking forth for the time of my coming, for it is nigh at hand. (D&C 35:13–15, emphasis added)

When I first read these verses as a young missionary in Samoa, I was somewhat offended. To think that the Lord would call me weak, simple, despised, and unlearned didn't seem very complimentary. However, when I looked more closely, I discovered His reasoning—He didn't want someone who was overly confident in his or her own abilities. He wanted those who knew they were unprepared so that He could then "thresh the nations by the power of [His] Spirit."

He knew you would be in peril among a rapidly deteriorating world, so He promised to defend you by His own arm as you "fight manfully for [Him]."

Hardly can a point be made more powerfully—don't stand in the way of people coming to Christ by trying to convert them to the messenger.

Why would people be drawn to the missionaries? The Lord answers that in Doctrine and Covenants 88:40:

> For intelligence cleaveth unto intelligence; wisdom receiveth wisdom; truth embraceth truth; virtue loveth virtue; light cleaveth unto light; mercy hath compassion on mercy and claimeth her own; justice continueth its course and claimeth its own; judgment goeth before the face of him who sitteth upon the throne and governeth and executeth all things.

Boiled down to its simplest form, that verse says, "Likes attract!" Not to jump too far ahead but so you don't miss the point, this is how you will eventually find your eternal companion. You incorporate the Christ-like traits and characteristics you want in an eternal companion into your own life, radiate those traits, and those who have similar traits will automatically be attracted to you.

How does that apply in missionary work? Because you live with yourself every day, you likely are not aware of what spirit you radiate. However, others who are not with you 24/7 are keenly aware of what you radiate. If they are seeking similar characteristics in their lives, they will be drawn to you.

Many times, they will mistake the spirit of the Holy Ghost which radiates from you as a personal appeal. Make sure you don't fall into the trap of thinking that it is because you are so wonderful that people can't stay away from you. Very often (especially with young elders and sisters), investigators will mistake the spirit you radiate—because you represent God, and 1 John 4:16 says that, "God is love"—as romantic attraction. Gently explain that the feeling they have mistaken for romantic love is actually them responding to the spirit of the Holy Ghost as you teach them.

If, after explaining what your investigator has mistakenly identified as romantic love, they are not willing to back off, call the mission president immediately. Don't assume you are safe because you are wearing a missionary badge.

President David O. McKay confirms what I have just written:

> There is one responsibility which no man can evade and that responsibility is his personal influence. Man's unconscious influence is the silent, subtle radiation of personality—the effect of his words and his actions on others. This radiation is tremendous. Every moment of life man is changing, to a degree, the life of the whole world.
>
> Every man has an atmosphere which is affecting every other man. He cannot escape for one moment from this radiation of his character. This constant weakening or strengthening of others. Man cannot evade the responsibility by merely saying that it is an unconscious influence.
>
> Man can select the qualities he would permit to be radiated. He can cultivate sweetness, calmness, trust, generosity, truth, justice, loyalty, nobility, and make them vitally active in his character. And by these qualities he will constantly affect the world.
>
> This radiation, to which I refer, comes from what a person really is, not from what he pretends to be. Every man by his mere living is radiating either sympathy, sorrow, morbidness, cynicism, or happiness and hope, or any one of a hundred other qualities.
>
> Life is a state of radiation and absorption. To exist is to radiate; to exist is to be the recipient of radiation. (*The*

> *Mission of Brigham Young University*, Brigham Young University Speeches of the Year [April 27, 1948])

One final word of caution: During your mission and throughout your life you may be the chosen instrument for delivering a powerful message from God to an individual or a group. You will receive many compliments on how wonderful a talk you've given was. Don't get too puffed up believing it is you or how wonderful you are (a problem with far too many missionaries and others). Joseph Smith said:

> When the Twelve or any other witnesses stand before the congregations of the earth, and they preach in the power and demonstration of the Spirit of God, and the people are astonished and confounded at the doctrine, and say, "That man has preached a powerful discourse, a great sermon," then let that man or those men take care that they do not ascribe the glory unto themselves, but be careful that they are humble, and ascribe the praise and glory to God and the Lamb; for it is by the power of the Holy Priesthood and the Holy Ghost that they have power thus to speak. What art thou, O man, but dust? And from whom receivest thou thy power and blessings, but from God? (*History of the Church*, 3:384)

It is a thrill that defies words to understand when the Lord singles you out to be His spokesman at any given time. Now you are sent to be His voice to a struggling world. Humbly accept His vote of confidence in your abilities—supplemented by His almighty power.

For your investigators:

Not infrequently you may be asked why you are teaching Christians. Then they follow up with, "Why don't you go to those who don't believe in Christ?" Don't be taken off guard with such an attack. In Doctrine and Covenants 1:2, 4–5, the Lord said:

> For verily the voice of the Lord is unto all men, and there is none to escape; and there is no eye that shall not see, neither ear that shall not hear, neither heart that shall not

> be penetrated. . . . And the *voice of warning shall be unto all people, by the mouths of my disciples*, whom I have chosen in these last days.
>
> And they shall go forth and none shall stay them, for I the Lord have commanded them (emphasis added).

Your commission to preach the gospel to the whole world—Christian and non-Christian—echoes what Christ told His ancient missionaries:

> Go ye therefore, and teach all nations, baptizing them in the name of the Father, and of the Son, and of the Holy Ghost:
>
> Teaching them to observe all things whatsoever I have commanded you: and, lo, I am with you alway, even unto the end of the world. (Matthew 28:19–20)

Then as a final follow-up, which may well open the door to your teaching, the Lord says:

> Wherefore, whithersoever they shall send you, go ye, and I will be with you; and in whatsoever place ye shall proclaim my name an effectual door shall be opened unto you, that they may receive my word. (D&C 112:19)

Explain, humbly, that you didn't call yourself as a missionary—it is a call from the Lord through His chosen prophet. Where you are sent to serve is also not a product of a choice you made but under the inspiration of heaven, you are sent where you are serving. Note also that you may, at the inspiration of the Church leaders, be moved at any time to any mission in the world. You are to serve where you are and not try to counsel the Lord where you think you ought to be.

Your full-time mission will end sooner than you know. Take full advantage of being a chosen vessel to bring all those whom the Spirit is preparing to join the Church into the fold of God. You will change their lives forever—but you will also enrich and change your life forever.

Chapter 11

Lord's Law of Witnesses

The law of witnesses has been a vital part of the Lord's method of operation from the very beginning of time. Paul taught the Corinthian saints: "In the mouth of two or three witnesses shall every word be established" (2 Corinthians 13:1).

Almost 2,500 years before the Book of Mormon was published Nephi saw the three witnesses and also the eight witnesses. He records:

> Wherefore, at that day when the book shall be delivered unto the man of whom I have spoken, the book shall be hid from the eyes of the world, that the eyes of none shall behold it save it be that three witnesses shall behold it, by the power of God, besides him to whom the book shall be delivered; and they shall testify to the truth of the book and the things therein.
>
> And there is none other which shall view it, save it be a few according to the will of God, to bear testimony of his word unto the children of men; for the Lord God hath said that the words of the faithful should speak as if it were from the dead. (2 Nephi 27:12–13)

Take the time to read the testimony of the Three Witnesses and the Eight Witnesses in the front of the Book of Mormon. Note that the Three Witnesses—Oliver Cowdery, David Whitmer, and Martin

Harris—testify that they saw the plates, saw the angel Moroni, and heard the voice of God testifying of the truthfulness of the Book of Mormon. That confirms what Nephi saw centuries before.

Also note that the Eight Witnesses did not claim any supernatural manifestations, but a straightforward seeing and hefting (lifting) the plates. This also confirms what Nephi saw when he said others would see the plates according to the will of God.

Skeptics who claim Joseph Smith was a wizard and conjured up the vision for the Three Witnesses, have a tough time with the testimony of the Eight Witnesses who claim no such miraculous manifestations. Each of the eleven Witnesses was commanded to testify to the world what they knew to be true—the Book of Mormon is the word of God.

You may already know that the Three Witnesses saw more than the Golden Plates. In Doctrine and Covenants 17:1 is listed five articles they saw:

> Behold, I say unto you, that you must rely upon my word, which if you do with full purpose of heart, you shall have a view of the plates, and also of the breastplate, the sword of Laban, the Urim and Thummim, which were given to the brother of Jared upon the mount, when he talked with the Lord face to face, and the miraculous directors which were given to Lehi while in the wilderness, on the borders of the Red Sea.

Then, as mentioned earlier in this book, the Lord Himself testifies of the truthfulness of the Book of Mormon. "And he [Joseph Smith] has translated the book, even that part which I have commanded him, and as your Lord and your God liveth it is true" (D&C 17:6).

The Lord clarifies why you, as a missionary, are to testify of the truthfulness of the gospel. After a rather exhaustive listing of things we are to study, He says:

> That ye may be prepared in all things when I shall send you again to magnify the calling whereunto I have called you, and the mission with which I have commissioned you.

> Behold, I sent you out to testify and warn the people, and it becometh every man who hath been warned to warn his neighbor.
>
> Therefore, they are left without excuse, and their sins are upon their own heads. (D&C 88:80–82)

The testimony you will bear will be have a powerful influence in the day of judgment against those who reject your witness. The Lord explained the role you (missionaries) will play at the judgment day:

> And in whatsoever house ye enter, and they receive you, leave your blessing upon that house.
>
> And in whatsoever house ye enter, and they receive you not, ye shall depart speedily from that house, and shake off the dust of your feet as a testimony against them.
>
> And you shall be filled with joy and gladness; and know this, that in the day of judgment you shall be judges of that house, and condemn them;
>
> And it shall be more tolerable for the heathen in the day of judgment, than for that house; therefore, gird up your loins and be faithful, and ye shall overcome all things, and be lifted up at the last day. (D&C 75:19–22).

It is difficult to image the confidence the Lord has in His called missionaries. It is equally as difficult to comprehend the weight the Lord puts on the testimony of His missionaries. Missionaries to judge the world! What a thought.

There are blessings associated with the testimony you bear. In Doctrine and Covenants 62:3, the Lord states (emphasis added): "Nevertheless, ye are blessed, for the testimony which ye have borne is recorded in heaven for the angels to look upon; and they rejoice over you, and *your sins are forgiven you.*"

Although we don't go on missions to ask "what's in it for me" (a subject discussed in an earlier chapter), there are glimpses of the rewards the Lord promises for those who are willing to risk the scorn and mocking of the worldly as they bear testimony of the restored gospel. One huge blessing is a promise of the forgiveness of sins.

At times (when you get a companion who may not be as motivated to serve as you are or who doesn't seem to care about being obedient to mission rules) you may wonder if it wouldn't be better if you left your companion in the apartment and went out alone. The answer is "*no*."

The Lord commands: "And ye shall go forth in the power of my Spirit, preaching my gospel, two by two, in my name, lifting up your voices as with the sound of a trump, declaring my word like unto angels of God" (D&C 42:6).

The Lord then outlines His law for teaching the gospel:

> Again I say unto you, that it shall not be given to any one to go forth to preach my gospel, or to build up my church, except he be ordained by some one who has authority, and it is known to the church that he has authority and has been regularly ordained by the heads of the church.
>
> And again, the elders, priests and teachers of this church shall teach the principles of my gospel, which are in the Bible and the Book of Mormon, in the which is the fulness of the gospel.
>
> And they shall observe the covenants and church articles to do them, and these shall be their teachings, as they shall be directed by the Spirit.
>
> And the Spirit shall be given unto you by the prayer of faith; and if ye receive not the Spirit ye shall not teach. (D&C 42:11–14)

Let's note the points the Lord makes:

1. You must be set apart by one having authority—that is the stake president in most cases.
2. You are to teach the principles of the gospel as found in the scriptures.
3. You must "practice what you preach" or in other words live the principles you are teaching the people.

4. You teach what the Spirit directs you to teach. Can you see how important it is to have the Spirit when you teach?
5. If you don't have the Spirit there, you shall not teach. Without the Spirit it is impossible for your investigator to understand what you are teaching.

Very carefully read 1 Corinthians 2:11–14. Especially verse 14 where it says they "cannot" understand and it will be "foolishness" to them.

Very practically speaking, you must stay with your companion at all times. Not only is your companion essential to bear testimony of the truths you are teaching, but he is also a protection against false accusers. More than a few missionaries have been sent home dishonorably because they left their companions and Satan was able to lure them into major transgressions. Other missionaries have been sent home because they were falsely accused but their credibility as missionaries was destroyed. Do not compromise on this rule—no matter what. If your companion leaves you and you can't find him, call the mission president immediately then find a member of the same gender and stay with him or her until your companion is located.

If you won't bear your testimony, don't go on a mission. We met an elder on our first round of zone conferences when I served as a mission president, who introduced himself by saying, "I don't preach, I don't pray, I don't bear my testimony. I'm here because if I wasn't here my companion couldn't do the work." As a new mission president, I was confident I could win him over. However, over the next eight months he succeeded in destroying every companionship he was in. He ruined the relationship the missionaries had with the members, and finally in a teaching appointment where Sister Bott was attending, he refused to bear his testimony.

When I confronted him as to whether he intended to ever become a real missionary, he defiantly repeated his initial introductory response, "I don't preach, I don't pray, I don't bear my testimony. I'm here because if I wasn't here my companion couldn't do the work." I informed him that the mission field was for missionaries and that our obligation was to bear testimony of the truths that the Lord had restored. I explained that he was at a crossroad. He could either start being a testimony bearing missionary or he could go home.

Rather surprised by my ultimatum he asked, “Are you sending me home?” I answered, “No, if you go home *you* will be sending yourself home.” He thought for about fifteen seconds, stiffened up, and said he wasn’t about to change. He was on the plane returning home the next day. Occupying a spot in a missionary companionship without being willing to perform as a missionary is not acceptable.

Throughout your life you will be privileged to bear your testimony about what you know to be true. The faster you can learn the principles and put them to the test, the quicker you will be able to have the Spirit testify to what you say (see again D&C 100:5–8).

For your investigators:

Because many people, both sincere and skeptical, will challenge how you know the Church is true, you need to understand what your testimony is based upon. The Savior said: “If any man will do his will, he shall know of the doctrine, whether it be of God, or whether I speak of myself” (John 7:17).

Your testimony of tithing will be much more powerful if you have paid your tithing. Your witness of the Word of Wisdom will likewise be more convincing if you are living the principles found in the Word of Wisdom. But how do you testify of the truthfulness of Joseph Smith First Vision? Your best explanation will come from Moroni’s challenge in Moroni 10:3–5:

> Behold, I would exhort you that when ye shall read these things, if it be wisdom in God that ye should read them, that ye would remember how merciful the Lord hath been unto the children of men, from the creation of Adam even down until the time that ye shall receive these things, and ponder it in your hearts.
>
> And when ye shall receive these things, I would exhort you that ye would ask God, the Eternal Father, in the name of Christ, if these things are not true; and if ye shall ask with a sincere heart, with real intent, having faith in

> Christ, he will manifest the truth of it unto you, by the power of the Holy Ghost.
>
> And by the power of the Holy Ghost ye may know the truth of all things.

In spite of your best efforts, and your most sincere, Spirit-filled testimony, there will be many who will refuse to accept your witness. You must understand that they are not rejecting you—they are rejecting the Savior. Go on your way rejoicing that you have fulfilled the Savior's command to teach all nations, bearing witness of the Godhead and the restored gospel. Your reward will not be less than if everyone you bore witness to accepted.

Joseph Smith made this remarkable statement:

> Avoid contentions and vain disputes with men of corrupt minds, who do not desire to know the truth. Remember that 'it is a day of warning, and not a day of many words.' If they receive not your testimony in one place, flee to another, remembering to cast no reflections, nor throw out any bitter sayings. If you do your duty, it will be just as well with you, as though all men embraced the Gospel. (*Teachings of the Prophet Joseph Smith*, 43)

As a final confirmation of the power of your testimony, the Savior said:

> But into whatsoever city ye enter, and they receive you not, go your ways out into the streets of the same, and say,
>
> Even the very dust of your city, which cleaveth on us, we do wipe off against you: notwithstanding be ye sure of this, that the kingdom of God is come nigh unto you.
>
> But I say unto you, that it shall be more tolerable in that day for Sodom, than for that city. (Luke 10:10–12)

Let the Spirit testify to you when the witness you have left is accounted by the Lord as their full chance. It is helpful if you leave praying that some other set of missionaries might be more effective in piquing their interest in the restored gospel. If the Spirit bears witness that they have received a full chance, you will know for sure what course of action you are to take. It is a very serious thing to seal your testimony against those who reject you.

President Joseph Fielding Smith gave this sobering thought:

> They [the missionaries] were to remember also that one important duty which they were to fulfill and that was to be sure and bear testimony in every instance. If they performed their labors sincerely, humbly and diligently bearing witness of the restoration, then it would be more tolerable for the heathen in the day of judgment, than for that house which rejected the message. If no warning had been left, however, then the judgment would be pronounced against the servant who was expected to deliver it. . . . The elders who delivered the message were also to be judges in the day of judgment against those who rejected their testimony. Missionaries of the Church should realize this fact. They are sent to warn the world and when they faithfully do their duty, they will stand as witnesses against those who reject them, but if they fail to perform their duty, then those unto whom the message should have been given, will stand up as accusers in their turn, and the unfaithful servants will be condemned. (*Church History and Modern Revelation,* 2:46–47)

Chapter 12

Repent or Suffer

Heavenly Father wants all of His spirit children to successfully return to His presence. However, since "no unclean thing can dwell with God" (1 Nephi 10:21), and since "all have sinned and come short of the glory of God" (Romans 3:23), there has to be a way of cleansing those who have transgressed. If you don't know you are doing wrong, how can you repent?

Before the Church was restored, the Lord enlarged the Saints understanding of the necessity of repenting. He said: "And surely every man must repent or suffer, for I, God, am endless" (D&C 19:4).

That may sound harsh at first reading, but when one stops to consider God's objective—to bring to pass the immortality and eternal life of man (see Moses 1:39), if God is going to accomplish His goal, mankind has two options: repent or suffer.

The whole of Doctrine and Covenants section 19 puts the eternal scales of justice in a perspective we cannot misunderstand. Although this section contains deep doctrine, it also contains great understanding. Through the years we have heard of "hell" as a place of "weeping, wailing, and gnashing of teeth" (see Alma 40:13, as one example) which described the conditions associated with paying for our own sins.

Graciously, the Lord explains (other than for the sons of perdition), that suffering won't last forever—it will have an end. However, He says it is "endless torment" and it is also called "eternal damnation," but He explains that these terms are used as motivators to urge people to repent (see verses 6 and 7).

Then the Lord explains what He terms a "mystery." He defines "endless punishment" as His punishment because "Endless is [His] name." It would be like saying, "It is Tom's Service Station" because Tom is the owner. The Lord then reiterates:

> For, behold, the mystery of godliness, how great is it! For, behold, I am endless, and the punishment which is given from my hand is endless punishment, for Endless is my name. Wherefore—
>
> Eternal punishment is God's punishment.
>
> Endless punishment is God's punishment. (D&C 19:10–12)

The punishment which is prepared for those who choose not to repent and take advantage of the cleansing power of Christ's Atonement is called Endless and Eternal because the Owner of the chamber where people will suffer belongs to Christ—and those are two of His names! It does not necessarily denote the amount of time a sinner will spend balancing the scales of eternal justice.

Many years ago, Apostle James E. Talmage gave a very enlightening talk on the purpose of having a "hell" and also the duration of the time people will spend in "hell."

> Hell is no place to which a vindictive judge sends prisoners to suffer and to be punished principally for his glory; but it is a place prepared for the teaching, the disciplining of those who failed to learn here upon the earth what they should have learned. True, we read of everlasting punishment, unending suffering, eternal damnation. That is a direful expression; but in his mercy the Lord has made plain what those words mean. "Eternal punishment" he says, is God's punishment, for he is eternal; and that condition or state or possibility will ever exist for the sinner who deserves and really needs such condemnation; but this does not mean that the individual sufferer or sinner is to be eternally and everlastingly made to endure and suffer. No

> man will be kept in hell longer than is necessary to bring him to a fitness for something better. When he reaches that stage, the prison doors will open and there will be rejoicing among the hosts who welcome him into a better state. The Lord has not abated in the least what he has said in earlier dispensations concerning the operation of this law and his gospel, but he has made clear unto us his goodness and mercy through it all, for it is his glory and his work to bring about the immortality and eternal life of man. (Conference Report, April 1930, 97).

In teaching us the desirability of repenting over trying to pay for our sins ourselves, the Savior graphically describes what He went through to make an atonement for our sins:

> Therefore I command you to repent—repent, lest I smite you by the rod of my mouth, and by my wrath, and by my anger, and your sufferings be sore—how sore you know not, how exquisite you know not, yea, how hard to bear you know not.
>
> For behold, *I, God, have suffered these things for all, that they might not suffer if they would repent;*
>
> But if they would not repent they must suffer even as I;
>
> Which suffering caused myself, even God, the greatest of all, to tremble because of pain, and to bleed at every pore, and to suffer both body and spirit—and would that I might not drink the bitter cup, and shrink—
>
> Nevertheless, glory be to the Father, and I partook and finished my preparations unto the children of men.
>
> Wherefore, I command you again to repent, lest I humble you with my almighty power; and that you confess your sins, lest you suffer these punishments of which I have spoken, of which in the smallest, yea, even in the least degree you have tasted at the time I withdrew my Spirit. (D&C 19:15–20, emphasis added)

If you have ever had a time when life was so dark and miserable that you didn't care to live another minute, you have tasted "in the least degree" what it is like to have the Spirit withdraw. In fact, the Savior said we can't even imagine how "sore" or how "exquisite" the suffering would be.

When we consider that "God, the greatest of all" bled at every pore (something that would cause any mortal to die immediately), we get some inkling of what that punishment would be like.

Some people who don't want to repent may try to rationalize that the "Merciful Jesus" would never exact such a terrible price for our sinning. But the Savior doesn't lie. He said:

> And it shall come to pass, because of the wickedness of the world, that I will take vengeance upon the wicked, for they will not repent; for the cup of mine indignation is full; for behold, my blood shall not cleanse them if they hear me not. (D&C 29:17)

Joseph Smith learned from translating the Book of Mormon that God could not ignore the demands of justice which He had established. If He did, He would "cease to be God."

> Therefore, according to justice, the plan of redemption could not be brought about, only on conditions of repentance of men in this probationary state, yea, this preparatory state; for except it were for these conditions, mercy could not take effect except it should destroy the work of justice. Now the *work of justice could not be destroyed; if so, God would cease to be God.*
>
> And thus we see that all mankind were fallen, and they were in the grasp of justice; yea, the justice of God, which consigned them forever to be cut off from his presence.
>
> And now, the plan of mercy could not be brought about except an atonement should be made; therefore *God himself atoneth for the sins of the world, to bring about the plan of mercy, to appease the demands of justice*, that God might be a perfect, just God, and a merciful God also.

> Now, repentance could not come unto men except there were a punishment, which also was eternal as the life of the soul should be, affixed opposite to the plan of happiness, which was as eternal also as the life of the soul. (Alma 42:13–16, emphasis added)

Amulek, convert and missionary companion of Alma, taught the apostate people of Ammonihah:

> And he shall come into the world to redeem his people; and he shall take upon him the transgressions of those who believe on his name; and these are they that shall have eternal life, and salvation cometh to none else.
>
> Therefore the wicked remain as though there had been no redemption made, except it be the loosing of the bands of death; for behold, the day cometh that all shall rise from the dead and stand before God, and be judged according to their works.
>
> Now, there is a death which is called a temporal death; and the death of Christ shall loose the bands of this temporal death, that all shall be raised from this temporal death. (Alma 11:40–42)

As you read the Book of Mormon and the Doctrine and Covenants, you will hear the pleading voice of the Savior saying, "Please take advantage of my suffering and my Atonement. If you choose not to repent, I cannot shield you from the justice of God."

In another chapter we will discuss repentance and forgiveness of sins. This chapter is to help you understand why repentance is necessary if you want to avoid suffering.

For your investigators:

Because of Bible references, the idea of "hell" being a place of torment will not be new. However, many Christians have chosen to view those references as figurative and not real. As you share with them the restored gospel, they will see that repentance is not only a good option but a necessary step if they want to avoid having to pay for their own sins.

Caution should be taken not to dwell too much on suffering but to use what you know to illuminate the benefits of repentance. Fear should not be incentive to serve God and repent—love is the great motivator.

People may claim that "hell" is a state of mind or a figure of speech and not a real place. The Lord revealed: "And, behold, there is a place prepared for them from the beginning, which *place is hell*" (D&C 29:38, emphasis added).

While it is true that "hell" described the mental suffering of those who do not repent, it is also a physical place where torment of all kinds are present. No one who takes the Lord's teachings seriously would risk being consigned to "hell" for a single minute. Repentance is by far the better choice.

Chapter 13

Sabbath Day and Fasting

The Lord, who knows all things (see D&C 38:2), explained His reason for restoring the Church through the Prophet Joseph Smith:

> Wherefore, I the Lord, knowing the calamity which should come upon the inhabitants of the earth, called upon my servant Joseph Smith, Jun., and spake unto him from heaven, and gave him commandments. (D&C 1:17)

We have already discussed many of the commandments. Now we will discuss the commandments given specifically targeted to help us avoid being overcome by the world. We cannot expect to be tainted by the stains of a fallen world and still be welcomed in the presence of a just and pure God. Remember: "No unclean thing can dwell with God" (1 Nephi 10:21).

What is the Lord's remedy for avoiding being polluted by the world? *The Sabbath Day.* A year and four months after restoring the Church, the Lord revealed:

> And that thou mayest more fully keep thyself unspotted from the world, thou shalt go to the house of prayer and offer up thy sacraments upon my holy day;
>
> For verily this is a day appointed unto you to rest from your labors, and to pay thy devotions unto the Most High;

> Nevertheless thy vows shall be offered up in righteousness on all days and at all times;
>
> But remember that on this, the Lord's day, thou shalt offer thine oblations [the act of making a religious offering] and thy sacraments unto the Most High, confessing thy sins unto thy brethren, and before the Lord.
>
> And on this day thou shalt do none other thing, only let thy food be prepared with singleness of heart that thy fasting may be perfect, or, in other words, that thy joy may be full. (D&C 59:9–13).

When God created the earth, He labored for six days. We do not know the exact length of time that was called "day" but there were six definite time periods included in the creation story.

Since God's objective is to help us become like Him, He instituted the Sabbath as a sign that we are striving to follow His example and keep His commandments.

When God revealed the Sabbath to the newly liberated Children of Israel who had been in slavery for many centuries, He used rather harsh tactics to teach them to obey.

> Speak thou also unto the children of Israel, saying, Verily my sabbaths ye shall keep: for it is a sign between me and you throughout your generations; that ye may know that I am the Lord that doth sanctify you.
>
> Ye shall keep the sabbath therefore; for it is holy unto you: every one that defileth it shall surely be put to death: for whosoever doeth any work therein, that soul shall be cut off from among his people.
>
> Six days may work be done; but in the seventh is the sabbath of rest, holy to the Lord: whosoever doeth any work in the sabbath day, he shall surely be put to death.
>
> Wherefore the children of Israel shall keep the sabbath, to observe the sabbath throughout their generations, for a perpetual covenant.

> *It is a sign between me and the children of Israel for ever*: for in six days the Lord made heaven and earth, and on the seventh day he rested, and was refreshed. (Exodus 31:13–17, emphasis added)

Although the death penalty is not imposed on those who break the Sabbath in our day, the principle that it is a holy day and a sign between God and His people is still very much in force. Being bombarded constantly with the evils of this world, we are commanded to keep the Sabbath day holy "lest thou forget the Lord" (see Deuteronomy 6:12).

Be careful not to fall into the trap of trying to make a list of what one can and can't do on the Sabbath. It is the principles behind the activities which should determine its acceptability.

The Lord's method for keeping us "unspotted from the world" is to go to the house of prayer (our chapels) and offer up our sacraments on His holy day. Since the Resurrection of Christ, the Saints have met on "the Lord's Day," which is Sunday. From Moses's day to the Resurrection, the Children of Israel met on the seventh day. There are places in the world where Latter-day Saints meet on a day other than Sunday. More important than the specific day is the fact that Latter-day Saints set apart one day a week to focus on their relationship with God.

Before partaking of the sacrament, we are to follow the apostle Paul's directive:

> For if we would judge ourselves, we should not be judged.
>
> But when we are judged, we are chastened of the Lord, that we should not be condemned with the world. (1 Corinthians 11:31–32)

If we would diligently review our thoughts, words, and actions of the past week and then resolve to make whatever corrections are necessary, we would not go very far astray in one week's time. People don't "fall into apostasy" they "slide and drift" until they are in a state of apostasy.

The Sabbath is the day specifically set apart to pay our devotions to the Lord, renew our covenants, and identify where adjustments must be made to align ourselves with the gospel. The Lord does remind us that we are to remember Him every day and at all times. If we could do that, we would never be in jeopardy of being overcome by the spotted and filthy world.

The Lord commands that even our food is to be prepared in a way not to distract from the spirit of worship on that holy day. In our day, many talks have been given by living prophets encouraging us to keep the Sabbath day holy. Some of our leaders have reemphasized Nehemiah's charge: "And if the people of the land bring ware or any victuals on the sabbath day to sell, that we would not buy it of them on the sabbath, or on the holy day" (Nehemiah 10:31). Though preparing food on the Sabbath is often unavoidable, it seems that preparing our food with singleness of heart is also a part of keeping the Sabbath holy.

A good principle for you to live by and also to teach others when they ask you about what is or is not admissible as a Sabbath day activity might be, "Be honest with yourself! If the proposed activity takes your focus away from the Lord and staying unspotted from the world, then it is not all right. If the proposed activity draws you back into the world, and makes it more difficult to focus on the Lord and His gospel, then don't do it!"

The promises for keeping the Sabbath day holy are outlined by Isaiah:

> If thou turn away thy foot from the sabbath, from doing thy pleasure on my holy day; and call the sabbath a delight, the holy of the Lord, honourable; and shalt honour him, not doing thine own ways, nor finding thine own pleasure, nor speaking thine own words:
>
> Then shalt thou delight thyself in the Lord; and I will cause thee to ride upon the high places of the earth, and feed thee with the heritage of Jacob thy father: for the mouth of the Lord hath spoken it. (Isaiah 58:13–14)

As the Lord continued His teaching the newly organized Church, He uses some interesting terminology. He says:

> And on this day thou shalt do none other thing, only let thy food be prepared with singleness of heart that thy fasting may be perfect, or, in other words, that thy joy may be full.

> Verily, this is fasting and prayer, or in other words, rejoicing and prayer. (D&C 59:13–14)

Unless children are taught the true purpose of the fast, many would not use the word "rejoicing" as a synonym for "fasting"! And yet the Lord commanded, as part of the parental responsibilities of Latter-day Saints: "And they shall also teach their children to pray, and to walk uprightly before the Lord. And the inhabitants of Zion shall also observe the Sabbath day to keep it holy" (D&C 68:28–29).

Also, in Doctrine and Covenants section 59, the Lord promises:

> And inasmuch as ye do these things with thanksgiving, with cheerful hearts and countenances, not with much laughter, for this is sin, but with a glad heart and a cheerful countenance—
>
> Verily I say, that inasmuch as ye do this, the fulness of the earth is yours, the beasts of the field and the fowls of the air, and that which climbeth upon the trees and walketh upon the earth;
>
> Yea, and the herb, and the good things which come of the earth, whether for food or for raiment, or for houses, or for barns, or for orchards, or for gardens, or for vineyards;
>
> Yea, all things which come of the earth, in the season thereof, are made for the benefit and the use of man, both to please the eye and to gladden the heart. (D&C 59:15–18)

It should be evident that the Lord has given us the Sabbath day as a blessing—not a commandment to stop us from having fun.

In today's world there are so many ways people can become addicted that it would take an entire volume to begin to list them. However, if Saints will observe the fast, those bonds can be broken. Returning to Isaiah 58, the Lord says: "Is not this the fast that I have chosen? to loose the bands of wickedness, to undo the heavy burdens, and to let the oppressed go free, and that ye break every yoke?" (Isaiah 58:6)

As you read through the scriptures, pay particular attention when fasting is mentioned. The Savior fasted for forty days before beginning

His mortal ministry. Often fasting is mentioned when a particular blessing is desired. In times of mourning, people fast and pray for the comfort of the Holy Ghost.

When one takes the focus off from the body and directs his thoughts towards God, the partnership of God and man becomes more real. We are then following the Lord's injunction:

> And again, verily I say unto you, my friends, I leave these sayings with you to ponder in your hearts, with this commandment which I give unto you, that ye shall call upon me while I am near—
>
> Draw near unto me and I will draw near unto you; seek me diligently and ye shall find me; ask, and ye shall receive; knock, and it shall be opened unto you.
>
> Whatsoever ye ask the Father in my name it shall be given unto you, that is expedient for you. (D&C 88:62–64)

For your investigators:

Fasting and Sabbath observance is taught in the Bible. However, many Christians have drifted away from the commandments and are currently paying the price for disobedience. You can help them get a clearer vision of the benefits of fasting and Sabbath observance, by taking the above scriptures and searching out the multitude of other scriptures found in the Bible to reinforce this commandment.

Chapter 14

Sacrament, Ordinances, and Covenants

Let's first make sure we understand what these terms mean:

> **Covenant:** An agreement between God and man, but they do not act as equals in the agreement. God gives the conditions for the covenant, and men agree to do what he asks them to do. God then promises men certain blessings for their obedience.
>
> Principles and ordinances are received by covenant. Members of the Church who make such covenants promise to honor them. For example, members covenant with the Lord at baptism and renew those covenants by partaking of the sacrament. They make further covenants in the temple. The Lord's people are a covenant people and are greatly blessed as they keep their covenants with the Lord. (Guide to the Scriptures, "Covenant," scriptures.lds.org)
>
> **Ordinances**: Sacred rites and ceremonies. Ordinances consist of acts that have spiritual meanings. Ordinances can also mean God's laws and statutes.

> Ordinances in the Church include administration to the sick (James 5:14–15), blessing the sacrament (D&C 20:77, 79), baptism by immersion (Matt. 3:16; D&C 20:72–74), blessing of children (D&C 20:70), conferring the Holy Ghost (D&C 20:68; 33:15), conferring the priesthood (D&C 84:6–16; 107:41–52), temple ordinances (D&C 124:39), and marriage in the new and everlasting covenant (D&C 132:19–20). (Guide to the Scriptures, "Ordinances," scriptures.lds.org)
>
> **Vicarious Ordinance:** A religious ordinance performed by a living person in behalf of one who is dead. These ordinances take effect only when those for whom the ordinances were performed accept them, keep the covenants associated with them, and become sealed by the Holy Spirit of Promise. Such ordinances are performed today within temples. (Guide to the Scriptures, "Ordinances," scriptures.lds.org)
>
> **Sacrament:** For Latter-day Saints, *sacrament* refers to the ordinance of partaking of bread and water in remembrance of Christ's atoning sacrifice. The broken bread represents His broken flesh; the water represents the blood that He shed to atone for our sins (1 Cor. 11:23–25; D&C 27:2).When worthy Church members take the sacrament, they promise to take upon them the name of Christ, to always remember Him, and to keep His commandments. Through this ordinance, Church members renew their baptismal covenants. (Guide to the Scriptures, "Sacrament," scriptures.lds.org)

During Old Testament times, under the Law of Moses, daily sacrifices and rituals were designed to keep the peoples' attention focused on God and keeping the commandments. Paul taught the role the Law of Moses played: "Wherefore the law was our schoolmaster to bring us unto Christ, that we might be justified by faith" (Galatians 3:24).

When the Savior came to work out His Atonement, He established ordinances and covenants as keys necessary to enter into the kingdom of God (see John 3:3–5). Baptism was that first key. The resurrected John the Baptist first conferred the power to baptize (i.e. the Aaronic Priesthood) on Joseph Smith and Oliver Cowdery, then commanded them to baptize each other. Carefully read Joseph Smith History 1:68–74.

Following baptism, the Holy Ghost is given. Those two ordinances (baptism and the conferral of the Holy Ghost) qualify a person to enter the celestial kingdom if they keep the commandments and endure to the end. Since we are prone to forget, the Lord instituted the sacrament—a weekly reminder that we are to "always remember Him and keep His commandments which He has given [us]" (D&C 20:77, 79).

If we would follow that simple pattern of weekly partaking of the sacrament and then always remembering what we covenanted to do when we were baptized, we would be able to "more fully keep thyself unspotted from the world" (D&C 59:9).

It is challenging now, and will be even more challenging in the future, to live in a sin-sick world and not become "spotted" by the world. The promise the Lord gives for us "always remembering Him" is that we "may always have His Spirit to be with [us]." If you are aware, you will note that it isn't difficult to resist temptation when you are in a spiritual fireside or meeting. It is when we are in situations that the Spirit is not with us that we have more difficulty avoiding temptations.

You may wonder why the Church doesn't use wine for the sacrament like the Savior did when He instituted the sacrament. Or you may serve your mission in a part of the world where something other than water is used. The Lord revealed:

> For, behold, I say unto you, that it mattereth not what ye shall eat or what ye shall drink when ye partake of the sacrament, if it so be that ye do it with an eye single to my glory—remembering unto the Father my body which was laid down for you, and my blood which was shed for the remission of your sins. (D&C 27:2).

The Lord outlines the prerequisites for a person (or your future investigators) to qualify for baptism:

> And again, by way of commandment to the church concerning the manner of baptism—All those who (1) humble themselves before God, and (2) desire to be baptized, and (3) come forth with broken hearts and contrite spirits, and (4) witness before the church that they have truly repented of all their sins, and (5) are willing to take upon them the name of Jesus Christ, (6) having a determination to serve him to the end, and (7) truly manifest by their works that they have received of the Spirit of Christ unto the remission of their sins, shall be received by baptism into his church. (D&C 20:37, numbers added)

Added to that list is what Alma taught his converts at the Waters of Mormon:

> And it came to pass that he said unto them: Behold, here are the waters of Mormon (for thus were they called) and now, (1) as ye are desirous to come into the fold of God, and (2) to be called his people, and (3) are willing to bear one another's burdens, that they may be light;
>
> Yea, and (4) are willing to mourn with those that mourn; yea, and (5) comfort those that stand in need of comfort, and (6) to stand as witnesses of God at all times and in all things, and in all places that ye may be in, even until death, that ye may be redeemed of God, and be numbered with those of the first resurrection, that ye may have eternal life—
>
> Now I say unto you, if this be the desire of your hearts, what have you against being baptized in the name of the Lord, as a witness before him that ye have entered into a covenant with him, (7) that ye will serve him and keep his commandments, that he may pour out his Spirit more abundantly upon you? (Mosiah 18:8–10, numbers added)

Before you rush to get an investigator baptized, make sure they understand what responsibilities they are taking upon themselves at baptism. It is also of upmost importance that you be striving to live according to the covenants you have made. Even though you will not be perfect, as you are striving diligently to keep your covenants, the Spirit will powerfully testify to your investigators that you are "walking the walk and not just talking the talk."

For your investigators:

Not infrequently you will hear people say, "I'm spiritual but I'm not religious." By that they imply that they can chart their own course and make up the rules for having and keeping the Spirit with them. However, when confronted with the Savior's statement to Nicodemus, their argument falls apart. He said:

> Verily, verily, I say unto thee, Except a man be born again, he cannot see the kingdom of God.
>
> Nicodemus saith unto him, How can a man be born when he is old? can he enter the second time into his mother's womb, and be born?
>
> Jesus answered, Verily, verily, I say unto thee, Except a man be born of water and of the Spirit, he cannot enter into the kingdom of God. (John 3:3–5)

Christ set up the Church to be the place where the ordinances are performed. Even some members of the Church (who lack understanding) will profess to believe they can just say the words "I marry you for time and all eternity" and have it be binding even though they do not go to the temple. We will discuss that idea more in the chapter on marriage and children.

Many investigators (not understanding the doctrine) will claim that they have already been baptized in their Church and shouldn't need to be baptized again when they join our Church. The Lord explained in Doctrine and Covenants 22:1–4:

> Behold, I say unto you that all old covenants have I caused to be done away in this thing; and this is a new

> and an everlasting covenant, even that which was from the beginning.
>
> Wherefore, although a man should be baptized an hundred times it availeth him nothing, for you cannot enter in at the strait gate by the law of Moses, neither by your dead works.
>
> For it is because of your dead works that I have caused this last covenant and this church to be built up unto me, even as in days of old.
>
> Wherefore, enter ye in at the gate [baptism], as I have commanded, and seek not to counsel your God. Amen.

Familiarize yourself with Acts 19:1–6, where twelve men claimed to have been baptized by John the Baptist's baptism but had not received the Holy Ghost. Paul baptized them again in the Savior's name and then gave them the Holy Ghost. This biblical example of the necessity of being baptized and confirmed by those holding the legitimate priesthood should help them understand why they need to be baptized.

Chapter 15

Prophetic Leadership and Scripture

This may be one of the most important chapters in this book for you and for your investigators. In the Lord's Preface to the Doctrine and Covenants (section 1), the Lord states:

> Search these commandments, for they are true and faithful, and the prophecies and promises which are in them shall all be fulfilled.
>
> What I the Lord have spoken, I have spoken, and I excuse not myself; and though the heavens and the earth pass away, my word shall not pass away, but shall all be fulfilled, whether by mine own voice or by the voice of my servants, it is the same. (D&C 1:37–38)

There are two very distinct parts to these verses. First is the command to study the scriptures—particularly the Doctrine and Covenants. The Savior gave the same command in John 5:39: "Search the scriptures; for in them ye think ye have eternal life: and they are they which testify of me."

Second is the declaration that whether by His own voice or the voice of His servants, it is the same. Perhaps that is one reason He gave this command on the very day the Church was restored:

> Wherefore, meaning the church, thou shalt give heed unto all his words and commandments which he shall give unto you as he receiveth them, walking in all holiness before me;
>
> For his word ye shall receive, as if from mine own mouth, in all patience and faith.
>
> For by doing these things the gates of hell shall not prevail against you; yea, and the Lord God will disperse the powers of darkness from before you, and cause the heavens to shake for your good, and his name's glory. (D&C 21:4–6)

For your benefit, and the future safety of your investigators, the Lord gave three promises to those who follow His chosen prophets:

1. "The gates of hell shall not prevail against you." What are the "gates of hell"? Unrepented sin will result in a person spending time in the hell portion of the spirit world to pay for his own sins. Therefore, by following the counsel and commandments of the living prophet, sin will never blindside you.
2. "The Lord God will disperse the powers of darkness from before you." That could mean that the veil of darkness Satan has succeeded in covering the world with (see Moses 7:26), thus preventing us from seeing things as God sees them, will be pushed aside by the teachings of the living prophets so that we are not deceived by the doctrine of devils in these last days.
3. The Lord will "cause the heavens to shake for your good, and his name's glory." I don't know how much power it takes to shake the earth but add to that the heavens and you can see that whatever power you need will be readily available if you follow the counsel of the living prophets.

As you would suspect, Satan will try to counterfeit the revelations from the Lord in order to deceive honest members of the Church and sincere seekers of truth. That happened five months after the Church was restored. Hiram Page, an early acquaintance of Joseph Smith and Oliver Cowdery, claimed to receive revelation through a stone he had found. The Lord said:

> But, behold, verily, verily, I say unto thee, no one shall be appointed to receive commandments and revelations in this church excepting my servant Joseph Smith, Jun., for he receiveth them even as Moses. (D&C 28:2)

Ten months after the Church was restored, a Mrs. Hubble came testifying that the Book of Mormon was true and claiming that she had been sent by the Lord as a teacher in the Church. The Lord responded by giving this revelation:

> And this ye shall know assuredly—that there is none other appointed unto you to receive commandments and revelations until he be taken, if he abide in me.
>
> But verily, verily, I say unto you, that none else shall be appointed unto this gift except it be through him; for if it be taken from him he shall not have power except to appoint another in his stead.
>
> And this shall be a law unto you, that ye receive not the teachings of any that shall come before you as revelations or commandments;
>
> And this I give unto you that you may not be deceived, that you may know they are not of me. (D&C 43:3–6)

The safety net the Lord has put in place is something you are very familiar with: The law of common consent. You may not know it by that name, but every time you are asked to sustain the prophet, apostles, general and local authorities, auxiliary leaders, teachers, etc. by raising your right hand, you acknowledge that those in authority have the right to initiate the call or act in the office they are ordained to. In Doctrine and Covenants 20:65, the Lord revealed: "No person is to be ordained to any office in this church, where there is a regularly organized branch of the same, without the vote of that church."

In Doctrine and Covenants 26:2, the Lord confirms what He taught in Section 20:65: "And all things shall be done by common consent in the church, by much prayer and faith, for all things you shall receive by faith."

Following the experience with Hiram Page, the Lord taught for the third time the importance of doing everything publicly, by common consent:

> For, behold, these things have not been appointed unto him, neither shall anything be appointed unto any of this church contrary to the church covenants.
>
> For all things must be done in order, and by common consent in the church, by the prayer of faith. (D&C 28:12–13)

There have been in the past, and will undoubtedly be more in the future, people coming forth and claiming to have had visions, visitations by angels, and revelations setting themselves up as leaders of the Church. Keep your eye on the First Presidency and the Quorum of the Twelve Apostles—they will never lead us astray.

Following the acceptance of the Manifesto doing away with plural marriage, President Wilford Woodruff made the following statement which is found at the end of the Doctrine and Covenants:

> The Lord will never permit me or any other man who stands as President of this Church to lead you astray. It is not in the programme. It is not in the mind of God. If I were to attempt that, the Lord would remove me out of my place, and so He will any other man who attempts to lead the children of men astray from the oracles of God and from their duty. (Official Declaration 1)

Others will come claiming that the First Presidency and the Quorum of the Twelve Apostles are at odds with what is written in the scriptures. The next portion of this chapter needs to be burned into your memory—you will need it.

President Wilford Woodruff gave a talk in the October 1897 General Conference. In part of that talk he said:

> I will refer to a certain meeting I attended in the town of Kirtland in my early days. At that meeting some remarks were made that have been made here today, with regard to the living prophets and with regard to the written word of God. The same principle was presented, although not as extensively as it has been here, when a leading man in the Church got up and talked upon the subject, and said: "You have got the word of God before you here in the Bible, Book of Mormon, and Doctrine and Covenants; you have the written word of God, and you who give revelations should give revelations according to those books, as what is written in those books is the word of God. We should confine ourselves to them." When he concluded, Brother Joseph turned to Brother Brigham Young and said, "Brother Brigham I want you to go to the podium and tell us your views with regard to the living oracles and the written word of God." Brother Brigham took the stand, and he took the Bible, and laid it down; he took the Book of Mormon, and laid it down; and he took the Book of Doctrine and Covenants, and laid it down before him, and he said: "There is the written word of God to us, concerning the work of God from the beginning of the world, almost, to our day." And now," said he, "when compared with the living oracles [prophets] those books are nothing to me; those books do not convey the word of God direct to us now, as do the words of a Prophet or a man bearing the Holy Priesthood in our day and generation. I would rather have the living oracles than all the writing in the books." That was the course he pursued. When he was through, Brother Joseph said to the congregation: "Brother Brigham has told you the word of the Lord, and he has told you the truth." (Conference Report, October 1897, 18–19)

In a talk given at Brigham Young University, President Ezra Taft Benson gave fourteen fundamental points for following the living prophet. His third point was:

> *The living prophet is more important to us than a dead prophet.*
>
> . . . God's revelations to Adam did not instruct Noah how to build the Ark. Noah needed his own revelation. Therefore, the most important prophet, so far as you and I are concerned, is the one living in our day and age to whom the Lord is currently revealing His will for us. Therefore, the most important reading we can do is any of the words of the prophet contained each month in our Church magazines. Our marching orders for each six months are found in the general conference addresses which are printed in the Ensign magazine. . . .
>
> Beware of those who would set up the dead prophets against the living prophets, for the living prophets always take precedence. ("Fourteen Fundamentals in Following the Prophet" [Brigham Young University devotional, February 26, 1980] speeches.byu.edu)

With regard to our priorities on who to follow, note the following: The New Testament explains the Old Testament—not visa versa. The Book of Mormon interprets the Bible. The Doctrine and Covenants interprets the Book of Mormon and living prophets explain, interpret, and enlarge all other scriptures. Once you understand this, most of the confusion that the anti-Mormons and the apostates cause is easily dismissed.

We live in a time when Satan has pulled out all the stops. He is using every evil device in his tool chest of dirty tricks to stop people from joining the Church and even more power is devoted to destroying the faith of members of the Church. As a missionary (and as an active lifelong member following your mission) you will have ample opportunities to help people understand what has been written in this chapter.

For your investigators:

Most Christians believe that prophets no longer walk the earth. Your testimony of the prophet Joseph Smith and living prophets today will undoubtedly be met with an array of opposition ranging from sincere questioning to hostile attacks. There seems to be some irony that Christians hold so tightly to the writings of dead prophets but refuse to accept living prophets.

Refer to Paul's account of what is the role of prophets and how long we will need them in the Church.

> And he gave some, apostles; and some, prophets; and some, evangelists; and some, pastors and teachers;
>
> For the perfecting of the saints, for the work of the ministry, for the edifying of the body of Christ:
>
> *Till we all come in the unity of the faith*, and of the knowledge of the Son of God, unto a perfect man, unto the measure of the stature of the fulness of Christ:
>
> That we henceforth be no more children, tossed to and fro, and carried about with every wind of doctrine, by the sleight of men, and cunning craftiness, whereby they lie in wait to deceive. (Ephesians 4:11–14, emphasis added)

What do prophets do? They are there for:

1. "The perfecting of the saints."
2. "For the work of the ministry." That includes, but is not limited to, missionary work.
3. "For the edifying of the body of Christ." Paul had referred to different members of the Church as parts of the "Body of Christ" (see 1 Corinthians 12:12–31). Part of the duties of Prophets and Apostles is to edify or spiritually build up the members of the Church.

How long will prophets and apostles be necessary in the Church? Paul taught:

1. "Till we all come in the unity of the faith." The fact that there are hundreds of Christian churches, each having some varying doctrine, would indicate that prophets and apostles are more necessary now that they were in Paul's day.
2. Until we come to "the knowledge of the Son of God." So far has Christianity drifted from the true knowledge of God and Christ, that our only hope for coming to know Them (which Christ defines as "life eternal": "And this is life eternal, that they might know thee the only true God, and Jesus Christ, whom thou hast sent" (John 17:3)) is through the teachings of living prophets and apostles.
3. Apostles and prophets are essential until we are instructed so we can come "unto a perfect man." Although the Savior marked the pathway leading to perfection, living prophets and apostles help us know how to continue our quest for perfection in these troubled times.
4. Our final destiny—to become exalted beings—is (in part) what is meant by us coming to "the measure of the stature of the fulness of Christ."

Paul understood that there would be an apostasy before the Second Coming. He taught:

> For I know this, that after my departing shall grievous wolves enter in among you, not sparing the flock.
>
> Also of your own selves shall men arise, speaking perverse things, to draw away disciples after them. (Acts 20:29–30)

He, therefore laid the responsibility upon the prophets and apostles to prevent us from being "children, tossed to and fro, and carried about with every wind of doctrine, by the sleight of men, and cunning craftiness, whereby they lie in wait to deceive."

Your message about living prophets and apostles will resonate in the ears of all of those who are currently prepared to join the Church. Others may reject you now but, at some future date, the satanic bombardment will soften them and they will remember your witness and seek out the Church. Harvest if they are ready. Plant and water if they are not ready yet.

Chapter 16

Protection for Missionaries and Saints

Too often members of the Church view themselves as being like any other person walking the face of the earth. However, the adversary doesn't view it that way. In Doctrine and Covenants 29:39, the Lord says that it is necessary for Satan to "tempt the children of men" (people who are not members of the Church—see Moses 8:20) but in Doctrine and Covenants 76:29, He states that Satan "maketh war with the saints of God, and encompasseth them round about." There is a significant difference between "being tempted" and being encompassed round about and having war waged against the Saints. However, the stakes are even higher when it comes to the missionaries.

While it is true that "every member is a missionary," many members do not go out of their way to be true member missionaries. However, as a "set apart" missionary, it is as though that black name tag you will wear appears in the adversary's sites as a bullseye.

You do not have to go forth to serve fearing and trembling for your life. The Lord said:

> Verily, thus saith the Lord unto you—there is no weapon that is formed against you shall prosper;

> And if any man lift his voice against you he shall be confounded in mine own due time.
>
> Wherefore, keep my commandments; they are true and faithful. (D&C 71:9–11)

How can you be expected to stand against an unseen enemy who has enjoyed over 6,000 years of experience destroying billions of God's spirit children? Without the warning and help from the Savior, you couldn't. Don't downplay the threat. The Lord told Joseph Smith and those associated with him who were spreading the gospel: ". . . behold, the enemy is combined. And now I show unto you a mystery, a thing which is had in secret chambers, to bring to pass even your destruction in process of time, and ye knew it not" (D&C 38:12–13).

Although caution is an imperative, you will enjoy protection that you cannot see. The Savior said: "But behold, verily, verily, I say unto you that mine eyes are upon you. I am in your midst and ye cannot see me" (D&C 38:7).

Then these comforting words: "And whoso receiveth you, there I will be also, for I will go before your face. I will be on your right hand and on your left, and my Spirit shall be in your hearts, and mine angels round about you, to bear you up" (D&C 84:88).

What can and must you do to prepare? The Lord repeats for our day a warning given by the ancient apostle Paul in Ephesians 6:11–18. In Doctrine and Covenants 27:15–18, the Lord tells us to put on the whole armor of God. Since Satan is at "war" with the Saints, armor is essential to win that battle.

> Wherefore, lift up your hearts and rejoice, and gird up your loins, and take upon you my whole armor, that ye may be able to withstand the evil day, having done all, that ye may be able to stand.
>
> Stand, therefore, having your loins girt about with truth, having on the breastplate of righteousness, and your feet shod with the preparation of the gospel of peace, which I have sent mine angels to commit unto you;

> Taking the shield of faith wherewith ye shall be able to quench all the fiery darts of the wicked;
>
> And take the helmet of salvation, and the sword of my Spirit, which I will pour out upon you, and my word which I reveal unto you, and be agreed as touching all things whatsoever ye ask of me, and be faithful until I come, and ye shall be caught up, that where I am ye shall be also.

Rather than taking a casual reading, let's identify each armor part and what it is to protect. First, we are to "stand having [our] *loins girt about with truth*." Why would the Lord start with the loins? Could it be that the loins, representing our reproductive abilities, would be the first and primary target of the adversary whose sole objective is to destroy you? What is the protective covering for the loins? *Truth*. What is truth, that if we have it, we will protect our virtue and chastity and without it we will not? The scriptural definition of truth is: "And truth is knowledge of things as they are, and as they were, and as they are to come" (D&C 93:24).

The truth is that the ability to procreate or have children is one factor that distinguishes our Heavenly Parents from any other beings in the eternal world. The truth is that we are here to be tested to see if we can use those godly powers of procreation as God commanded. The truth is that if we fail to control those powerful, God-given urges here in mortality, we put in jeopardy having those powers restored to our resurrected bodies in the eternal world. Only those in the highest degree of the celestial kingdom will have to power to have eternal increase (see D&C 131:1–4).

Another truth is that too many young men and women want to marry someone who has kept themselves clean and pure, yet they excuse their own inappropriate activities while dating. The truth is that it is total hypocrisy to expect your future mate to maintain a higher level of chastity than you maintain. So, if you don't want your future spouse to act inappropriately on a date—don't you act inappropriately on your dates. Using that standard while you are dating would all but eliminate immorality among the Latter-day Saints.

The next piece of armor we must put on is "the *breastplate of righteousness*." The breastplate covers our vital organs, specifically our heart. What is "righteousness"? There may be many definitions, but one easy way is to define what is "right." Can we agree that whatever God says is right is right and whatever He says is wrong is wrong? With that agreement we can readily see whether we have on the breastplate or not. If we are doing what God says to do, the breastplate is firmly in place. If we want to "pick and choose" which scriptural directives and prophetic counsels to live, the breastplate, if there at all, is ajar. If we openly rebel against the prophet's counsel, it is like going into a battle with no breastplate—pretty foolish.

If we would use the breastplate as defined, we would never become addicted to drugs or alcohol—the prophets have repeatedly warned us against using them. We would never become addicted to pornography—again frequently warned against—if we never view it the first time. If we use clean language, we never need be embarrassed when someone we respect hears us let out a string of profanity. If we never allow the social media to dominate our lives, we would never need worry about being totally unprepared when our mission age comes. If we never fight and quarrel with parents or siblings, we would never have to worry very much about getting along with a mission companion or a future spouse. You can see the list can be enlarged to encompass all of the tactics Satan is so successfully using at this time.

Next is the admonition to have your "*feet shod* with the preparation of the gospel of peace." What are the feet used for? To take us towards our goals. If your goal is the highest degree of the celestial kingdom where "naught but peace, justice, and truth is the habitation of thy throne" (Moses 7:31) exists, then it should be easy to make eternity-determining decisions correctly. You only need to ask, "If I do, or say, or act that way, will it take me closer to my eternal goal or will it be a detour that I know I will eventually have to correct?" One very good measuring stick is the temple recommend questions. If you can truthfully answer those questions, which constitute the minimum qualifications necessary to enter the temple, then you are on your way to the highest degree of the celestial kingdom. The Lord would not have one set of standards to enter His House (the temples are called

"The House of the Lord") and a whole different standard to enter His eternal home.

Next let's consider the "*helmet of salvation,*" since it is part of the body armor. The helmet protects our brain or our intellect. How does "salvation" protect that? Satan will never be able to destroy you until he destroys your belief in the plan of salvation. It isn't until you no longer accept that you are a child of God, and that you have the potential to grow and develop to become like Him, that the enticements of the world cause you to compromise your standards.

The plan of salvation gives you the reason and the strength to withstand the lure of the world. When Satan succeeds in destroying that vision of who you are, why you are on earth, and what lies ahead in eternity, then, domino-like, all of the other restraints fall away. Addictions destroy your agency, morality becomes (as the world sees it) old fashioned and out of date. Far too many Latter-day Saints (young and old) have allowed themselves to be overcome by the temptations of the devil and have ended up "hitting the bottom." Some pay the price to climb out of the bottomless pit and rejoined the Saints on the strait and narrow path leading back to the presence of God. Far too many fall prey to Satan's lie that they have gone beyond the point of no return and are lost forever.

The next part of the armor of God is the "*shield of faith* wherewith ye shall be able to quench *all* the fiery darts of the wicked." Where do you use a shield in a battle? Where you are being attacked! If your testimony of the plan of salvation is under attack—put the shield where it can cover your head as a reinforcement. If you are tempted to compromise your standards concerning the word of wisdom or your family relationship, put your shield over your breastplate. If you are being sorely tempted to break the law of chastity, put the shield over your loins. If you have lost your vision of what you want eternally and are being tempted to violate commandments which would disqualify you from entering the temple, put the shield over your feet. What do the scriptures say about using that shield of faith (in Christ) to overcome Satan's temptations? "Teach them to withstand every temptation of the devil, with their faith on the Lord Jesus Christ" (Alma 37:33).

There is one part of the anatomy which is not covered by the whole armor of God—the back! Perhaps the Lord is telling us that we cannot turn and run away from the battle but must meet it face-on. But even if we have all of the armor on, we will still lose the battle because we have no offensive weapon to destroy the adversary. What is that offensive weapon? "*The sword of the Spirit*, which I will pour out upon you, and my word which I reveal unto you." That is a two-edged sword. One is the Spirit which the Lord promises to pour out upon you as you serve, and second is His word which He promises to reveal to you. He promises:

> Therefore, verily I say unto you, lift up your voices unto this people; speak the thoughts that I shall put into your hearts, and you shall not be confounded before men;
>
> For it shall be given you in the very hour, yea, in the very moment, what ye shall say. (D&C 100:5–6)

The only way I know for you not to be worried about the wickedness of the world around you is to have on the whole armor of God.

Now, not only does God promise protection for His missionaries, He also promises protection for their families. To Joseph Smith and Sidney Rigdon who were on a mission and worried about their families, the Lord said: "Verily, thus saith the Lord unto you, my friends Sidney and Joseph, your families are well; they are in mine hands, and I will do with them as seemeth me good; for in me there is all power" (D&C 100:1).

Not a bad trade—your devotion to your missionary calling in exchange for the Savior's promise to take care of your families with His omnipotent power.

With a daily check on our armor, we can make what adjustments are necessary to ensure that when the battle comes—and it will come—we will be sufficiently prepared. If you have failed to prepare already in one or more areas, repent, pick yourself up, and re-enter the battle. God is counting on you not to fail. He needs you on His winning team.

For your investigators:

Sometime during a casual teaching experience it might be well to review with them the whole armor of God. If they are already well on their way to conversion, you can used Doctrine and Covenants 27:15–18. If they still have a ways to go before they are ready to commit to baptism, take them to Ephesians 6:11–18. It would be too bad if you failed to share with them the Lord's revealed key on how to "withstand in the evil day, and having done all, to stand" (Ephesians 6:13).

The Second Coming will be addressed in a future chapter, but these verses fit nicely into the protection for you and the Saints:

> And it shall be called the New Jerusalem, a land of peace, a city of refuge, a place of safety for the saints of the Most High God;
>
> And the glory of the Lord shall be there, and the terror of the Lord also shall be there, insomuch that the wicked will not come unto it, and it shall be called Zion.
>
> And it shall come to pass among the wicked, that every man that will not take his sword against his neighbor must needs flee unto Zion for safety.
>
> And there shall be gathered unto it out of every nation under heaven; and it shall be the only people that shall not be at war one with another.
>
> And it shall be said among the wicked: Let us not go up to battle against Zion, for the inhabitants of Zion are terrible; wherefore we cannot stand.
>
> And it shall come to pass that the righteous shall be gathered out from among all nations, and shall come to Zion, singing with songs of everlasting joy. (D&C 45:66–70)

Chapter 17

Adversity, Trials, and Tribulations

One word of caution as we begin this chapter: Don't think you understand the divine purpose behind everything that happens to you and others. You will see (and possibly experience yourself) suffering that seems to have no purpose. The Lord said:

> For verily I say unto you, blessed is he that keepeth my commandments, whether in life or in death; and he that is faithful in tribulation, the reward of the same is greater in the kingdom of heaven.
>
> *Ye cannot behold with your natural eyes, for the present time, the design of your God concerning those things which shall come hereafter*, and the glory which shall follow after much tribulation.
>
> For after much tribulation come the blessings. Wherefore the day cometh that ye shall be crowned with much glory; the hour is not yet, but is nigh at hand.
>
> Remember this, which I tell you before, that you may lay it to heart, and receive that which is to follow. (D&C 58:2–5, emphasis added)

The first point to keep in mind is that it isn't what challenges you or others face that matters, it is how you react to the tribulation that determines whether the problem wears you down or polishes you up.

Scattered throughout the Doctrine and Covenants are references to persecutions and trials. We will only be able to sample a few but as you prayerfully read the scriptures, your understanding will deepen. Then you will become the conduit through which comfort comes to your family, friends, and investigators.

Although you may never be called to lay down your life for your membership in the Church, some of you might. Almost a year before the Church was restored, the Lord told Joseph Smith: "And that you be firm in keeping the commandments wherewith I have commanded you; and if you do this, behold I grant unto you eternal life, *even if you should be slain*" (D&C 5:22, emphasis added).

Three years following the Church's restoration, the Lord hinted at others who would give their lives in His service, the purpose for the trial, and also the reward they would receive if they were faithful.

> For he will give unto the faithful line upon line, precept upon precept; and I will try you and prove you herewith.
>
> And whoso layeth down his life in my cause, for my name's sake, shall find it again, even life eternal.
>
> Therefore, be not afraid of your enemies, for I have decreed in my heart, saith the Lord, that I will prove you in all things, whether you will abide in my covenant, even unto death, that you may be found worthy.
>
> For if ye will not abide in my covenant ye are not worthy of me. (D&C 98:12–15)

Some people become angry with the Lord because of the bad things that happen to them. Others actually turn away from the Lord and His Church claiming that if there really was a God and He was a loving being, He would never let anything like this happen to them. It might be well to remind them that the Savior didn't deserve any of the persecution and trials He faced throughout His life but, through His suffering, He learned obedience and was made perfect (see Hebrews 5:8).

If you prayerfully read the entire Doctrine and Covenants, you will find more than a dozen reasons why bad things happen to good people. Only one will be the result of transgressions. In Section 101:2–5, the Lord says (emphasis added):

> I, the Lord, have suffered the affliction to come upon them, wherewith *they have been afflicted, in consequence of their transgressions*;
>
> Yet I will own them, and they shall be mine in that day when I shall come to make up my jewels.
>
> Therefore, they must needs be chastened and tried, even as Abraham, who was commanded to offer up his only son.
>
> For all those who will not endure chastening, but deny me, cannot be sanctified.

When a trial comes upon you or your acquaintances, pause and see if you have brought it upon yourselves by breaking a commandment or foolish actions on your part. For example, it would be unreasonable to accuse God if you were free-climbing and injured yourself in a fall.

However, part of the trials comes as the Lord prepares you for exaltation. No one will likely be asked to sacrifice his son, like Abraham was, as a manifestation of his faithfulness, but there are principles in that story which may help us understand.

1. Abraham was asked to do something he did not want to do.
2. Abraham was asked to give up something he loved very much.
3. Abraham was asked to do something he did not fully understand.
4. Abraham was asked to do something that went against his core beliefs.

Perhaps knowing at least those four principles included in Abraham's sacrifice of Isaac may help you or an investigator endure the trial without losing faith.

How does the Lord want us to react to trials? In Doctrine and Covenants 78:17–19, He states (emphasis added):

> Verily, verily, I say unto you, ye are little children, and ye have not as yet understood how great blessings the Father hath in his own hands and prepared for you;
>
> And ye cannot bear all things now; nevertheless, *be of good cheer*, for I will lead you along. The kingdom is yours and the blessings thereof are yours, and the riches of eternity are yours.
>
> And *he who receiveth all things with thankfulness* shall be made glorious; and the things of this earth shall be added unto him, even an hundred fold, yea, more.

Note how the Lord acknowledges that we are like little children in our understanding of eternal things. He also tells us that we are not going to pass every test 100% and that we will make mistakes. However, He reassures us that in spite of our weaknesses and stumblings, we are to be of good cheer. Don't get discouraged. Then the promises: He will lead us along. He promises us that the kingdom (both the Church on earth and the celestial kingdom) are within our reach. Even the riches of eternity are ours—which is earlier described as eternal life (see D&C 11:7).

Before giving the last blessing, the Lord gives a challenge which is often very difficult to do: "He who receiveth all things with thankfulness"—it is easy to thank the Lord when good things happen to us. However, when bad things happen, how can we be thankful? We will wait for the next section to answer that question. But if we can learn to give thanks in all things, the promises are that we shall be made glorious and receive the things of this earth even one hundred times what we otherwise would have received. That means physical and temporal blessings; but remember that the destiny of this earth is to become our celestial kingdom (see D&C 88:17–19, 25–26).

Following the expulsion of the Saints from Jackson County, Missouri, the Lord gives this comfort, commandment, and promise:

> Verily I say unto you my friends, fear not, let your hearts be comforted; yea, rejoice evermore, and in everything give thanks;
>
> Waiting patiently on the Lord, for your prayers have entered into the ears of the Lord of Sabaoth, and are recorded with this seal and testament—the Lord hath sworn and decreed that they shall be granted.
>
> Therefore, he giveth this promise unto you, with an immutable covenant that they shall be fulfilled; and all things wherewith you have been afflicted shall work together for your good, and to my name's glory, saith the Lord. (D&C 98:1–3)

His comfort was first to call us His friends. Next, not to be afraid (which we will explain in the next section). Third, let our hearts be comforted. Fourth, "rejoice evermore, and in everything give thanks." How can we rejoice and give thanks when bad things happen to us? Wouldn't that be hypocritical? Yes, it would be unless we can stand far enough back from the trial and see the lessons we have learned, the growth we have experienced, and that the positive things greatly outweigh the pain and suffering we have endured. Then we can truly give thanks for the bad things that happen to us.

Then the Lord urges us to be patient. Our prayers, which seem not to be answered, have been heard by divine ears and have received a promise—they (the pleadings in our prayers) will be fulfilled.

Then, as a confirmation that eventually our prayers will be answered, the Lord says He gives the promise of the fulfillment of our prayers with "an immutable covenant" (one that can't be changed or broken), and then adds something that mankind cannot cause to be fulfilled: "all things wherewith you have been afflicted shall work together for your good [which seems to indicate during our mortal life], and to my name's glory [which He says is to bring about your immortality and exaltation—Moses 1:39], saith the Lord."

Although there are many, many other scriptures explaining trials, afflictions, and tribulations, we will take just one more. The prophet Joseph Smith and several others had spent months in a cold, dungy, filthy dungeon in Liberty, Missouri. Sections 121, 122, and 123 are part of a longer letter he wrote from that jail. The first part seems to be Joseph's pleading with the Lord for some understanding and relief as to why they were allowed to be incarcerated that long.

However, the part that deals with the subject of this chapter is found in Doctrine and Covenants 122:7–9:

> . . . know thou, my son, that all these things shall give thee experience, and shall be for thy good.
>
> The Son of Man hath descended below them all. Art thou greater than he?
>
> Therefore, hold on thy way, and the priesthood shall remain with thee; for their bounds are set, they cannot pass. Thy days are known, and thy years shall not be numbered less; therefore, fear not what man can do, for God shall be with you forever and ever.

First the Lord says that all these problems will be to the eternal benefit of those who suffer. Then the Lord seems to say, "You want the same exaltation I have but are reluctant to have your own personal Gethsemane. And My Gethsemane was infinitely more difficult than yours!" Then the counsel: "Hold on thy way." He is saying, "Don't get discouraged, don't quit, don't think of committing suicide, hang in there. My power or the priesthood will not depart from you even under the worst of situations. Please know that their bounds (both the persecutors and the persecutions) are set—they cannot pass. They will not take your life before your assigned days in mortality are complete (see D&C 121:25). You are in My hands. Don't worry about what men can do. I will be with you forever and ever!"

Promises don't get any better than that.

For your investigators:

There seems to be no shortage of suffering in a world rapidly spiraling towards destruction. If you believe the scriptures, world conditions will get worse before they get better. Look for people who are suffering: people who have lost a loved one, people who are enduring sickness, people who have suffered financial setbacks, people who have problems within their marriages and with their children, people who are suffering from mental or physical ailments—the list is almost as endless as is mankind. Then offer your insight on the purposes behind the challenges we face in mortality. You may be the source of helping them see that suicide is not an acceptable means of escape from the trials of life. Although it seems trite, this statement is true: "Suicide is a permanent solution to a temporary problem." Lead people to Christ and let Him help them through their darkest hours.

First you must learn to accept trials without complaining before you can help others. So, start today being more trusting in the Lord's wisdom, knowing that He will not make you suffer longer or more than is absolutely necessary for your eternal exaltation. Then practice before your mission discussing with your family and loved ones the purposes behind our mortal trials. The more experience you have talking these things through before your mission, the easier it will be when you are the sole mortal source of comfort leading people to Christ through their personal Gethsemanes.

Chapter 18

Repentance and Forgiveness

One of the frequently used and most effective tools of the devil is to convince people who are really trying to live righteous lives that they have sinned to the point that they are not candidates for the celestial kingdom. That is just one more reason he is called "a liar from the beginning" (see D&C 93:25).

With that near constant whispering saying we have gone beyond the point of no return, far too many people, Latter-day Saints and preparing missionaries included, feel unworthy to claim the blessings promised by the Lord to those who are sincerely trying to keep the commandments.

When the Lord outlined the spiritual gifts available to help us perfect ourselves, He said:

> Wherefore, beware lest ye are deceived; and that ye may not be deceived seek ye earnestly the best gifts, always remembering for what they are given;
>
> For verily I say unto you, they are given for the benefit of those who love me and keep all my commandments, and *him that seeketh so to do*; that all may be benefited that seek or that ask of me, that ask and not for a sign that they may consume it upon their lusts. (D&C 46:8–9, emphasis added)

If we only read the first part of those who qualify for the spiritual gifts designed to help us avoid deception, we can easily get discouraged since they are given "for the benefit of those who love me and *keep all of my commandments*". However, if you are trying to keep the commandments, you are worthy for the divine help that comes through the gifts of the Spirit.

The Lord commands us to repent 628 times in the scriptures. In the Bible, the command is given 112 times, 363 times in the Book of Mormon, 129 times in the Doctrine and Covenants, and 24 times in the Pearl of Great Price.

Since another chapter is entitled "Repent or Suffer," why is this chapter necessary? We need to be very familiar with the Lord's invitation to repent leading us to a state of forgiveness where we can qualify for all the blessings the Lord has promised to the faithful.

What is real repentance? The Guide to the Scriptures states:

> A change of mind and heart that brings a fresh attitude toward God, oneself, and life in general. Repentance implies that a person turns away from evil and turns his heart and will to God, submitting to God's commandments and desires and forsaking sin. True repentance comes from a love for God and a sincere desire to obey His commandments. All accountable persons have sinned and must repent in order to progress toward salvation. Only through the Atonement of Jesus Christ can our repentance become effective and accepted by God. (Guide to the Scriptures, "Repent, Repentance," scriptures.lds.org)

In the very first section of the Doctrine and Covenants, the Lord explains the necessity of repenting:

> For I the Lord cannot look upon sin with the least degree of allowance;
>
> Nevertheless, he that repents and does the commandments of the Lord shall be forgiven;

> And he that repents not, from him shall be taken even the light which he has received; for my Spirit shall not always strive with man, saith the Lord of Hosts. (D&C 1:31–33)

Repentance is not an optional exercise. If we want to remain faithful members of the Lord's Church we must repent: "Thou knowest my laws concerning these things are given in my scriptures; he that sinneth and repenteth not shall be cast out" (D&C 42:28).

Repenting, as a prerequisite for baptism, is linked to our receiving a remission of our sins: "Repent and be baptized in the name of Jesus Christ, according to the holy commandment, for the remission of sins" (D&C 49:13).

You are going into a very dangerous world. The people you teach and members you encourage live permanently in that world. How can you be assured of protection? The Lord said: "And if your brethren desire to escape their enemies, let them repent of all their sins, and become truly humble before me and contrite" (D&C 54:3).

There have been many formulas given outlining the steps for repentance. The explanation by the Lord is the clearest and most definite:

> Behold, he who has repented of his sins, the same is forgiven, and I, the Lord, remember them no more.
>
> By this ye may know if a man repenteth of his sins—behold, he will *confess* them and *forsake* them. (D&C 58:42–43, emphasis added)

Confess, according to the magnitude of your sin, to the Lord, to yourself, to the one you have offended, and—if your sin puts in jeopardy your membership in the Church—the bishop. Confessing to others seems to give a temporary relief from the burden of guilt but before long the adversary is dredging up your sin and throwing it back in your face. Permanent relief comes when you comply with the Lord's command to confess to the appropriate people.

Forsake means not to do it again—ever. Is it likely that you may fall back into transgression in spite of your most diligent efforts? Yes. Does that mean you haven't really repented or that you haven't been forgiven? No.

The Lord told Alma how to handle repeat transgressors:

> Therefore I say unto you, Go; and whosoever transgresseth against me, him shall ye judge according to the sins which he has committed; and if he confess his sins before thee and me, and repenteth in the sincerity of his heart, him shall ye forgive, and I will forgive him also.
>
> Yea, and *as often as my people repent* will I forgive them their trespasses against me.
>
> And ye shall also forgive one another your trespasses; for verily I say unto you, he that forgiveth not his neighbor's trespasses when he says that he repents, the same hath brought himself under condemnation. (Mosiah 26:29–31, emphasis added)

The Lord's comment in the final verse above leads us to another very important concept: *forgive to be forgiven.*

To Joseph Smith, the Lord said:

> My disciples, in days of old, sought occasion against one another and forgave not one another in their hearts; and for this evil they were afflicted and sorely chastened.
>
> Wherefore, I say unto you, that ye ought to forgive one another; for he that forgiveth not his brother his trespasses standeth condemned before the Lord; for there remaineth in him the greater sin.
>
> I, the Lord, will forgive whom I will forgive, but of you it is required to forgive all men.
>
> And ye ought to say in your hearts—let God judge between me and thee, and reward thee according to thy deeds.
>
> And him that repenteth not of his sins, and confesseth them not, ye shall bring before the church, and do with him as the scripture saith unto you, either by commandment or by revelation.
>
> And this ye shall do that God may be glorified—not because ye forgive not, having not compassion, but that

> ye may be justified in the eyes of the law, that ye may not offend him who is your lawgiver—
>
> Verily I say, for this cause ye shall do these things. (D&C 64:8–14)

Because of the importance of this principle, we will analyze each verse, one at a time. In verse 8 the Lord revealed that there were hard feelings and wrongs committed by His early disciples. They dutifully told each other that they forgave but in their hearts they continued to hold grudges. The Lord explained that not only was that an "evil" but it resulted in their being "afflicted and sorely chastened."

Can we expect less if we mouth the words forgiving those who have wronged us but we continue to harbor ill feelings within?

Verse 9 has been the subject of much discussion among the Latter-day Saints. How, if we withhold forgiveness, do we come under greater condemnation than the person who has sinned? There are many possible explanations, we will take only one.

Your role as a missionary is to bring souls to Christ. Don't ever stand in between your investigator and the Savior who, with His fullness of knowledge knows all of the conditions leading up to their sinning, knows all they have gone through, knows the condition of their heart, and knows what the future will hold. You know none of that.

When you withhold forgiveness, it is like you stepping between the sinner and the Savior. Taking a preeminent position to the Lord is, by scriptural definition, *blasphemy* (see John 10:33)—that is a greater sin than anything the sinner may have done to you.

In verse 10, the Lord plainly states that forgiveness is something He judges when and where the sinner is to receive. He doesn't invite us to assist or assume the role of judge. Therefore, He says, "Don't worry, I will take care of judgment. That is a burden too heavy for you to carry."

In verse 11, the Lord goes so far as to tell us how to handle the situation, "Just say in your heart—I'm going to forgive you—no strings attached. I will leave to the Lord the burden of judgment. I have a life to live and a future to prepare for. I don't have time to allow what you have done to me the power to stop my spiritual progress."

Then verses 12–14 are given to priesthood leaders how to proceed with the sinner who is unwilling to repent. By following this course of action, we put ourselves in a position to receive forgiveness from the Lord. You needn't worry, the Lord will balance the eternal scales of justice perfectly, if not immediately or even during mortality, at least in the eternal worlds. Here is how the Lord explained eventual justice:

> But wo unto them that are deceivers and hypocrites, for, thus saith the Lord, I will bring them to judgment.
>
> Behold, verily I say unto you, there are hypocrites among you, who have deceived some, which has given the adversary power; but behold such shall be reclaimed;
>
> But the hypocrites shall be detected and shall be cut off, either in life or in death, even as I will; and wo unto them who are cut off from my church, for the same are overcome of the world. (D&C 50:6–8).

How can you tell when you have been forgiven, or on the pathway to being forgiven, of your sins? Satan will tell you that you can never be forgiven and you are only indulging in wistful thinking. Let's discuss a few principles that will help you and your investigators realize when your sins have been washed away.

The easiest principle to understand comes from the Lord's explanation on how we can recognize when we are on a course leading to the celestial kingdom. In Doctrine and Covenants 111:8, He said; "And the place where it is my will that you should tarry, for the main, shall be signalized unto you by the peace and power of my Spirit, that shall flow unto you."

As long as we are on the right track and moving forward according to the Lord's timetable, He signalizes that by peace and the power (or presence) of His Spirit. If we deviate from that course, He alerts us that we are heading in the wrong direction by the withdrawal of His spirit. If we have unrepented sins, the Spirit cannot dwell with us. So, when the Spirit is there, it is a manifestation that we have been forgiven.

Let's add to that vital key. King Benjamin gave a powerful sermon that an angel had delivered to him concerning the Savior. Then, Mormon records:

> And now, it came to pass that when king Benjamin had made an end of speaking the words which had been delivered unto him by the angel of the Lord, that he cast his eyes round about on the multitude, and behold they had fallen to the earth, for the fear of the Lord had come upon them.
>
> And they had viewed themselves in their own carnal state, even less than the dust of the earth. And they all cried aloud with one voice, saying: O have mercy, and apply the atoning blood of Christ that we may receive forgiveness of our sins, and our hearts may be purified; for we believe in Jesus Christ, the Son of God, who created heaven and earth, and all things; who shall come down among the children of men.
>
> And it came to pass that after they had spoken these words the Spirit of the Lord came upon them, and they were *filled with joy*, having received a remission of their sins, and having *peace of conscience*, because of the exceeding faith which they had in Jesus Christ who should come, according to the words which king Benjamin had spoken unto them. (Mosiah 4:1–3, emphasis added)

They were "filled with joy" and enjoyed "peace of conscience." Later in chapter 5, the people testified: "The Spirit of the Lord Omnipotent, which has wrought a mighty change in us, or in our hearts, that we have *no more disposition to do evil, but to do good continually*" (Mosiah 5:2, emphasis added).

A further testimony concerning forgiveness is given by Alma the Younger. You recall that he and the sons of King Mosiah had done all in their power to destroy the church of God. An angel had called them up short. After three days and nights of repenting "nigh unto death," Alma was "born again" and experienced a remission of his sins (see Mosiah 27:8–31 for the whole story).

A generation later, Alma was teaching his sons. He still had a very vivid memory of his experience with the angel and repentance but one thing was missing:

> Now, as my mind caught hold upon this thought [about the Son of God—see verse 17], I cried within my heart: O Jesus, thou Son of God, have mercy on me, who am in the gall of bitterness, and am encircled about by the everlasting chains of death.
>
> And now, behold, when I thought this, *I could remember my pains no more; yea, I was harrowed up by the memory of my sins no more.*
>
> And oh, what joy, and what marvelous light I did behold; yea, my soul was filled with joy as exceeding as was my pain!
>
> Yea, I say unto you, my son, that there could be nothing so exquisite and so bitter as were my pains. Yea, and again I say unto you, my son, that on the other hand, there can be nothing so exquisite and sweet as was my joy. (Alma 36:18–21, emphasis added)

Some well-meaning but uninformed members may suggest that when you have been forgiven of your sins that you won't remember them. That is not a true statement. The torment will be gone but the memory will still be there.

Will the adversary try to throw former sins in your face in order to discourage and destroy you? Absolutely—plan on it. Then, like the Savior, you can, with confidence say, "Get thee behind me Satan" (Luke 4:8).

Remember Moses 6:60 where the Lord says (in part): "By the Spirit ye are justified." To be justified means you are not under divine condemnation. It means you are living as well as the Lord expects you to given the amount of light and knowledge you have. It means you have been forgiven of your sins or are qualifying for forgiveness.

It would be a totally mixed message if the Lord left His Spirit with you and you hadn't been forgiven of your sins. He would be testifying of your acceptance of Him at the same time knowing that your unrepented sins would bar you from reentering His presence.

To your investigators (and you!):

Remember that the Lord taught:

> For if ye forgive men their trespasses, your heavenly Father will also forgive you:
>
> But if ye forgive not men their trespasses, neither will your Father forgive your trespasses. (Matthew 6:14–15)

Far too many Latter-day Saints have quit attending church because someone has offended them. Whether the offense is real or not really doesn't matter. Why would they give the offender the power to rob them of the joy and progress that comes from full church involvement? The same is true for non-members. Spouses, family members, neighbors, and former friends all suffer when we fail to follow the Lord's admonition to "forgive all men."

You have a unique role in helping to heal the hurt, mend the social fences, and move the Saints and the people of the world to a much more happy and peaceful state. First make sure you have completely and totally forgiven all who have wronged you. Then you are in a position to help others do the same.

A word of explanation: Perhaps an explanation to help you understand what appears to be a contradiction between Alma's teaching about the Lord forgiving every time we repent and Doctrine and Covenants 82:7, which reads: "And now, verily I say unto you, I, the Lord, will not lay any sin to your charge; go your ways and sin no more; but unto that soul who sinneth shall the former sins return, saith the Lord your God."

Sin is a willful transgression of the law (see 3 Nephi 6:18). It is easily visualized if you consider that all your shadowy, sinful past is behind you as long as you face the sun (or the Son of God). Even though we stumble and fall occasionally (or frequently), as long as we are facing the Son, our former sins do not return. It isn't until we turn our back on the Son and willfully sin that all our former sins return by being illuminated by the radiance of His Being.

Chapter 19

The Word of Wisdom

In discussing the Word of Wisdom in this chapter, make sure you understand that the *Word of Wisdom is not the entire gospel.* Over forty years of teaching college age students and also thousands of adults, it is disappointingly prevalent when people want to make differences in dietary preferences the divisive factor in the Church. We should be reminded that the word "wisdom" is mentioned 378 times in the scriptures. Only eight times is it used exclusively referring to what we eat or drink. Four of those references are in Section 89. Two in the Old Testament, once in the Book of Mormon, and the other in Doctrine and Covenants 27.

Becoming fanatical in areas of food is not a new challenge. Paul wrote to the Corinthians: "And every man that striveth for the mastery is temperate in all things" (1 Corinthians 9:25).

Being over-zealous was a problem even in Book of Mormon times. Alma encourages members of the Church:

> And now my beloved brethren, I have said these things unto you that I might awaken you to a sense of your duty to God, that ye may walk blameless before him, that ye may walk after the holy order of God, after which ye have been received.

> And now I would that ye should be humble, and be submissive and gentle; easy to be entreated; full of patience and long-suffering; being temperate in all things; being diligent in keeping the commandments of God at all times; asking for whatsoever things ye stand in need, both spiritual and temporal; always returning thanks unto God for whatsoever things ye do receive.
>
> And see that ye have faith, hope, and charity, and then ye will always abound in good works.
>
> And may the Lord bless you, and keep your garments spotless, that ye may at last be brought to sit down with Abraham, Isaac, and Jacob, and the holy prophets who have been ever since the world began, having your garments spotless even as their garments are spotless, in the kingdom of heaven to go no more out. (Alma 7:22–25)

Before going to the Doctrine and Covenants, let's take a look at Paul's counsel to the Roman Saints:

> Him that is weak in the faith receive ye, but not to doubtful disputations.
>
> For one believeth that he may eat all things: another, who is weak, eateth herbs.
>
> Let not him that eateth despise him that eateth not; and let not him which eateth not judge him that eateth: for God hath received him.
>
> Who art thou that judgest another man's servant? to his own master he standeth or falleth. Yea, he shall be holden up: for God is able to make him stand.
>
> One man esteemeth one day above another: another esteemeth every day alike. Let every man be fully persuaded in his own mind.
>
> He that regardeth the day, regardeth it unto the Lord; and he that regardeth not the day, to the Lord he doth not regard it. He that eateth, eateth to the Lord, for he giveth

God thanks; and he that eateth not, to the Lord he eateth not, and giveth God thanks.

For none of us liveth to himself, and no man dieth to himself.

For whether we live, we live unto the Lord; and whether we die, we die unto the Lord: whether we live therefore, or die, we are the Lord's.

For to this end Christ both died, and rose, and revived, that he might be Lord both of the dead and living.

But why dost thou judge thy brother? or why dost thou set at nought thy brother? for we shall all stand before the judgment seat of Christ.

For it is written, As I live, saith the Lord, every knee shall bow to me, and every tongue shall confess to God.

So then every one of us shall give account of himself to God.

Let us not therefore judge one another any more: but judge this rather, that no man put a stumblingblock or an occasion to fall in his brother's way.

I know, and am persuaded by the Lord Jesus, that there is nothing unclean of itself: but to him that esteemeth any thing to be unclean, to him it is unclean.

But if thy brother be grieved with thy meat, now walkest thou not charitably. Destroy not him with thy meat, for whom Christ died.

Let not then your good be evil spoken of:

For the kingdom of God is not meat and drink; but righteousness, and peace, and joy in the Holy Ghost.

For he that in these things serveth Christ is acceptable to God, and approved of men.

> Let us therefore follow after the things which make for peace, and things wherewith one may edify another.
>
> For meat destroy not the work of God. All things indeed are pure; but it is evil for that man who eateth with offence.
>
> It is good neither to eat flesh, nor to drink wine, nor any thing whereby thy brother stumbleth, or is offended, or is made weak.
>
> Hast thou faith? have it to thyself before God. Happy is he that condemneth not himself in that thing which he alloweth.
>
> And he that doubteth is damned if he eat, because he eateth not of faith: for whatsoever is not of faith is sin.
>
> We then that are strong ought to bear the infirmities of the weak, and not to please ourselves.
>
> Let every one of us please his neighbour for his good to edification. (Romans 14:1–15:2)

Perhaps as well as any chapter in scripture, Paul puts into proper perspective how the Word of Wisdom ranks with other principles that are significantly more important in the eternal scheme of things.

The actual Word of Wisdom begins in the Section before 89, where the bulk of the revelation is located. In Section 88, the Lord teaches:

> See that ye love one another; cease to be covetous; learn to impart one to another as the gospel requires.
>
> Cease to be idle; cease to be unclean; cease to find fault one with another; cease to sleep longer than is needful; retire to thy bed early, that ye may not be weary; arise early, that your bodies and your minds may be invigorated.
>
> And above all things, clothe yourselves with the bond of charity, as with a mantle, which is the bond of perfectness and peace. (D&C 88:123–125)

Those issues have as much or more to do with our developing Christ-like attributes than those dietary cautions given in Section 89. Consider the impact if we cannot learn to live together in love. There would be no eternal marriages, no "forever families," no united wards or neighborhoods. We may be the healthiest people in the world, but if we cannot get along, we have nothing. As you consider the other instructions of the Lord, you will see that He is focusing more on attributes essential to celestial living than on health issues.

Why was the Word of Wisdom given? The Lord answers: It was given "by revelation and the word of wisdom, showing forth the order and will of God in the temporal salvation of all saints in the last days" (D&C 89:2).

The Lord knew what conditions would exist in our day leading up to the Second Coming. He warned: "In consequence of evils and designs which do and will exist in the hearts of conspiring men in the last days, I have warned you, and forewarn you, by giving unto you this word of wisdom by revelation" (D&C 89:4).

The Lord knew that evil people more interested in gain than in the worth of souls would promote drugs, alcohol, tobacco, and other harmful substances in spite of the devastation those substances would have on individual, marriages, and families.

The Lord begins His cautionary list with alcohol. He knew we would be succored into becoming a world of alcoholics and therefore said drinking alcohol or strong drinks "is not good."

After explaining the proper use of wine and strong drinks, He turns His attention to tobacco. Since we are not "sick cattle," tobacco isn't "good for either the body or the belly." Basically, it really has no place in the life of an aspiring Saint.

Next, the Lord cautions against "hot drinks." This was interpreted by Hyrum Smith (brother of the prophet Joseph Smith) as being "tea and coffee." Since they are good neither for the body or belly, we would be wise to stay away from them. You will undoubtedly find people (both inside the Church and outside) that want to argue about hot chocolate, iced tea, and other drinks that contain harmful substances. It is wisdom on your part to avoid such arguments. Very likely no one will change their opinion based on your arguments. Teach them to be sensitive to the presence or absence of the Spirit to determine the rightness or wrongfulness of any substance.

In verse 10, the Lord reveals that "wholesome herbs" are good for the use of man. Verses 10–17 taken together state that grains are to constitute the "staff of life" other than in times of winter, cold, or famine where meat can be the mainstay of the diet. Once again, debating on how much meat is to be used is a fruitless argument.

You need to be aware that in Doctrine and Covenants 49:18–19 the Lord revealed (emphasis added):

> And whoso forbiddeth to abstain from meats, that man should not eat the same, is not ordained of God;
>
> For, behold, the beasts of the field and the fowls of the air, and that which cometh of the earth, is ordained for the use of man for food and for raiment, and that *he might have in abundance*."

A better gauge of how much meat is too much would be the presence or absence of the Spirit (consider carefully D&C 111:8). Too often arguments and contentions arise which cause the Spirit to withdraw. Far too many Latter-day Saints view the Word of Wisdom as restrictive rather than as a loving Heavenly Father's attempt to help us live long healthy lives, avoiding the pitfalls that accompany those substances He warns us against.

Focus on the promised blessings found in verse 18–21:

> And all saints who remember to keep and do these sayings, walking in obedience to the commandments, shall receive health in their navel and marrow to their bones;
>
> And shall find wisdom and great treasures of knowledge, even hidden treasures;
>
> And shall run and not be weary, and shall walk and not faint.
>
> And I, the Lord, give unto them a promise, that the destroying angel shall pass by them, as the children of Israel, and not slay them.

Those Saints and investigators who are more anxious about pleasing the Lord than debating with Him, will find greater health and more peace than those who continue to try to get the Lord to change His mind on those substances. The only official addition that has been made to the Word of Wisdom since it was given in 1833 is the addition of "harmful drugs" not mentioned in 1833 because they were not in existence.

For your investigators:

Although the revelation called the Word of Wisdom (D&C 89) is unique to the restored gospel, Romans 14 and 1 Corinthians 10:23–33 provide a perfect opportunity to discuss the Lord's interest in our physical wellbeing. Share Doctrine and Covenants 89 in the context of Romans 14 and if you refuse to argue specific amounts and individual products, much can be gained by helping them understand that living healthily only adds more strength to their efforts to live a more Christ-like life.

Chapter 20

Tithing and the Law of Consecration

Tithing is defined by the Lord in Doctrine and Covenants 119:4 as "those who have thus been tithed shall pay one–tenth of all their interest annually." "Interest" has been defined by latter-day prophets as "income." This is a freewill offering. It is not a doctrine unique to Latter-day Saints. Through His prophet, Malachi, the Lord said:

> Will a man rob God? Yet ye have robbed me. But ye say, Wherein have we robbed thee? In tithes and offerings.
>
> Ye are cursed with a curse: for ye have robbed me, even this whole nation.
>
> Bring ye all the tithes into the storehouse, that there may be meat in mine house, and prove me now herewith, saith the Lord of hosts, if I will not open you the windows of heaven, and pour you out a blessing, that there shall not be room enough to receive it.
>
> And I will rebuke the devourer for your sakes, and he shall not destroy the fruits of your ground; neither shall your vine cast her fruit before the time in the field, saith the Lord of hosts. (Malachi 3:8–10)

This is a challenge and a promise that we cannot afford to overlook in bringing ourselves and our investigators to Christ. The Lord challenges us to "bring our tithes and offerings" to—in our day—the bishop. He then promises to "open the windows of heaven and pour you out a blessing that there shall not be room enough to receive it."

In today's world, where poverty is more the norm than an exception, this is one way of proving our trust in the Lord and His promised blessings. The strength of your testimony will be magnified if you were a full tithe payer before your mission.

Tithing has been a principle from the very earliest times. Abraham paid tithes to Melchizedek of one-tenth of all that he had (see Genesis 14:20). Moses and the Children of Israel also lived the law of tithing (see Leviticus 27:30–31). Tithing was being paid during Christ's day (see Luke 18:11–12). The resurrected Savior taught the law of tithing to the Nephites (see 3 Nephi 24:8–12).

Even before the law of tithing was formally given in our day, the Lord explained part of the power and protection that comes to those who faithfully pay their tithes:

> Behold, now it is called today until the coming of the Son of Man, and verily it is a day of sacrifice, and a day for the tithing of my people; for he that is tithed shall not be burned at his coming.
>
> For after today cometh the burning—this is speaking after the manner of the Lord—for verily I say, tomorrow all the proud and they that do wickedly shall be as stubble; and I will burn them up, for I am the Lord of Hosts; and I will not spare any that remain in Babylon. (D&C 64:23–24)

Although tithing has often been jokingly referred to as "fire insurance," at the Second Coming it will be no joking matter. Why would those who are tithed not be burned at the Second Coming? Perhaps it is because the thing the world values most is wealth. If a person is willing to voluntarily give up ten percent of his income, it would indicate that he has overcome the spirit of greed so prevalent in the world. Then tithing becomes an outward manifestation of an inward testimony that the Lord comes first, that the lure of the world has been overcome, and that a person is willing to sacrifice whatever the Lord commands in order to enjoy the promised protection.

Some people will want to know whether you pay on your "gross income" (i.e. before taxes are taken out) or on your "net income" (i.e. after taxes are taken out). Since tithing is a free-will offering, the Bishop will not ask whether you are tithing on the gross or the net. He will merely ask: "Is this a full tithing?" Your answer is between you and the Lord.

One Church leader many years ago was asked the "gross verse net" question. After some thought he said: "If I want 'gross' blessings, I pay on the gross income. If I want 'net' blessings I pay on the net income" (see Charles W. Penrose, "Is This Plain Enough?" in *Handbook of the Restoration*, ed. Zion's Printing & Publishing [Montana: Kessinger Publishing, 2007], 458). That is something to consider but it is not the doctrine of the Church.

Another Church leader some years ago, when asked how he calculated tithing said, "I set up a hypothetical situation in my mind. Supposing that the Lord said, "Because of a surplus in My storehouse, I have decided to give every faithful member ten percent of their income as a reward for faithfulness. You sit down and figure out what the Lord will pay you, then you, in turn, pay that to the Lord as your tithing" (see James E. Talmage, in Conference Report Oct. 1928, 119). That is an interesting way of looking at tithing—but again that is not the doctrine of the Church but something to consider. Tithing really is between you and God.

Many faithful tithe payers will testify that it is impossible to get the Lord in your debt. In other words, you can't pay yourself poor when it comes to paying tithing. King Benjamin, in his final address to his people said it this way:

> I say unto you that if ye should serve him who has created you from the beginning, and is preserving you from day to day, by lending you breath, that ye may live and move and do according to your own will, and even supporting you from one moment to another—I say, if ye should serve him with all your whole souls yet ye would be unprofitable servants.

> And behold, all that he requires of you is to keep his commandments; and he has promised you that if ye would keep his commandments ye should prosper in the land; and he never doth vary from that which he hath said; therefore, if ye do keep his commandments he doth bless you and prosper you.
>
> And now, in the first place, he hath created you, and granted unto you your lives, for which ye are indebted unto him.
>
> And secondly, he doth require that ye should do as he hath commanded you; for which if ye do, he doth immediately bless you; and therefore he hath paid you. And ye are still indebted unto him, and are, and will be, forever and ever; therefore, of what have ye to boast? (Mosiah 2:21–24)

Although you will likely never teach the law of consecration (sometimes referred to as "the United Order"), you should be aware that someday, if we are faithful in paying our tithes, we will be permitted by the Lord to share all things in common.

The city of Enoch, before they were translated and taken off the earth, lived that law of consecration. Moses 7:18 records: "And the Lord called his people Zion, because they were of one heart and one mind, and dwelt in righteousness; and there was no poor among them." They lived much longer then than we do now. So likely we will not live long enough to be translated, as they were.

Shortly after the Lord ascended into heaven, the Saints in His day were living the law of consecration. "And the multitude of them that believed were of one heart and of one soul: neither said any of them that ought of the things which he possessed was his own; but they had all things common" (Acts 4:32).

Following the resurrected Lord's visit to the Nephites they began an unparalleled time of peace and prosperity. Mormon records: "And they had all things common among them; therefore there were not rich and poor, bond and free, but they were all made free, and partakers of the heavenly gift" (4 Nephi 1:3).

In our day, the Lord gave the basics of the law of consecration. In Doctrine and Covenants 42:30–34, the Lord revealed:

> And behold, thou wilt remember the poor, and consecrate of thy properties for their support that which thou hast to impart unto them, with a covenant and a deed which cannot be broken.
>
> And inasmuch as ye impart of your substance unto the poor, ye will do it unto me; and they shall be laid before the bishop of my church and his counselors, two of the elders, or high priests, such as he shall appoint or has appointed and set apart for that purpose.
>
> And it shall come to pass, that after they are laid before the bishop of my church, and after that he has received these testimonies concerning the consecration of the properties of my church, that they cannot be taken from the church, agreeable to my commandments, every man shall be made accountable unto me, a steward over his own property, or that which he has received by consecration, as much as is sufficient for himself and family.
>
> And again, if there shall be properties in the hands of the church, or any individuals of it, more than is necessary for their support after this first consecration, which is a residue to be consecrated unto the bishop, it shall be kept to administer to those who have not, from time to time, that every man who has need may be amply supplied and receive according to his wants.
>
> Therefore, the residue shall be kept in my storehouse, to administer to the poor and the needy, as shall be appointed by the high council of the church, and the bishop and his council.

Then in Doctrine and Covenants 51:2–3, the Lord further instructed how that equality was to exist among the saints:

> For it must needs be that they be organized according to my laws; if otherwise, they will be cut off.
>
> Wherefore, let my servant Edward Partridge, and those whom he has chosen, in whom I am well pleased, appoint unto this people their portions, every man equal according to his family, according to his circumstances and his wants and needs.

Because of selfishness and greed, the Lord withdrew the privilege of living the law of consecration. However, at some time in the future, we must learn to live the law,

> That you may be equal in the bonds of heavenly things, yea, and earthly things also, for the obtaining of heavenly things.
>
> For if ye are not equal in earthly things ye cannot be equal in obtaining heavenly things;
>
> For if you will that I give unto you a place in the celestial world, you must prepare yourselves by doing the things which I have commanded you and required of you. (D&C 78:5–7)

Finally, the Lord said: "And Zion cannot be built up unless it is by the principles of the law of the celestial kingdom; otherwise I cannot receive her unto myself" (D&C 105:5).

Much of what I have just written will likely go beyond your present level of understanding or interest. However, as you serve your mission, return home, and continue active Church membership, you will read the Doctrine and Covenants and discover that the Lord has revealed a great deal about the law of consecration that will be lived by those in the celestial kingdom.

For your investigators:

I would not discuss the law of consecration with your investigators. It is mentioned here only because you may be asked by members in your mission about the "United Order" or the "law of consecration" and I did not want you to be totally clueless about what they are talking about.

However, you must teach the law of tithing since that is the law under which members of the Church live in our day. Using the above scriptures, teach the blessings that come from faithful payment of tithes rather than focusing on the sacrifices necessary to pay tithing. Paying tithing is a sacrifice only to those who fail to recognize the blessings which they receive. Those blessings far outweigh the sacrifice of giving back to the Lord 10% of what He gives to them on a daily basis.

Chapter 21

The Second Coming of Christ

One topic that piques the interest of both members and non-members alike is the rapidly approaching Second Coming of Christ. Ironically, the term "Second Coming" is only mentioned once in the scriptures.

> And more blessed are you because you are called of me to preach my gospel—
>
> To lift up your voice as with the sound of a trump, both long and loud, and cry repentance unto a crooked and perverse generation, preparing the way of the Lord for his second coming. (D&C 34:5–6)

Isn't it interesting that a call to missionary service is associated with the only place the actual words "Second Coming" is used? We are blessed to be members of the Lord's true Church, but "more blessed" because of our call as missionaries.

There are so many sections of the Doctrine and Covenants dealing with the Second Coming that it would take many volumes to fully list and discuss what is contained therein. A word of caution before we start our discussion: Stick with what has been written in the scriptures and taught by Latter-day prophets. Far too many members and non-members listen to every fantastic rumor that floats around. Many of those rumors are not true. Your best and safest course is to keep your eye on the living prophet. Remember what Amos taught: "Surely the Lord God will do nothing, but he revealeth his secret unto his servants the prophets" (Amos 3:7).

If you are in a conversation where speculation is out of control, either change the subject or remove yourself from the conversation. Be very careful what you say because everything you will say (as a missionary) will be taken as gospel truth.

Not to overwhelm you, but so you have the information available, here are the sections of the Doctrine and Covenants where the majority of the Second Coming information is contained: 29, 38, 43, 45, 63, 88, 101, 133, and Joseph Smith—Matthew.

Two quick notes before we start our discussion: 1. The signs of the times are given to prepare us and not to scare us (see D&C 38:30—"If ye are prepared, ye shall not fear"); 2. As you read these sections, carefully note the difference between what is happening among the wicked in the world and what is described as the condition of the Saints. It is true that terrible things will happen to the wicked but the righteous can and will escape most of the devastation. As an example, Doctrine and Covenants 97:21 states: "Therefore, verily, thus saith the Lord, let Zion rejoice, for this is Zion—the pure in heart; therefore, *let Zion rejoice, while all the wicked shall mourn.*" What are "the pure in heart" doing? Rejoicing. What are all the wicked doing? Mourning. You and all mankind have a clear choice—become pure in heart and rejoice or keep doing wicked things and mourn.

The most frequently asked question is: "When will the Second Coming happen?" While it is true that "I, the Lord God, have spoken it; but the hour and the day no man knoweth, neither the angels in heaven, nor shall they know until he comes" (D&C 49:7), there are some broad guidelines signaling the approach.

Doctrine and Covenants section 77 is a Question and Answer by the Lord on certain passages from the Book of Revelation in the Bible. In verse 6, it states:

> Q. What are we to understand by the book which John saw, which was sealed on the back with seven seals?
>
> A. We are to understand that it contains the revealed will, mysteries, and the works of God; the hidden things of his

> economy concerning this earth during the seven thousand years of its continuance, or its temporal existence.

We know it will be approximately 7,000 years from Adam's day to the end of the Millennium. The Bible Dictionary (see page 635) places the Fall of Adam at approximately 4000 B.C.

The Millennium is defined as 1,000 years. That would place the opening of the 7th seal at approximately 2000 A.D.—a date already passed. However, in Doctrine and Covenants 77:12–13, the following information is explained (emphasis added):

> Q. What are we to understand by the sounding of the trumpets, mentioned in the 8th chapter of Revelation?
>
> A. We are to understand that as God made the world in six days, and on the seventh day he finished his work, and sanctified it, and also formed man out of the dust of the earth, even so, in the beginning of the seventh thousand years will the Lord God sanctify the earth, and complete the salvation of man, and judge all things, and shall redeem all things, except that which he hath not put into his power, when he shall have sealed all things, unto the end of all things; and the sounding of the trumpets of the seven angels are the preparing and finishing of his work, in the beginning of the seventh thousand years—the preparing of the way before the time of his coming.
>
> Q. When are the things to be accomplished, which are written in the 9th chapter of Revelation?
>
> A. They are to be accomplished *after the opening of the seventh seal, before the coming of Christ.*"

How long that period will be isn't revealed. We could very well be in that space now. Read Revelation 9 and see what is described. Keep in mind that in 1831 the Lord said: "Prepare ye, prepare ye for that which is to come, for the Lord is nigh" (D&C 1:12). How long will it be? We don't know, but we know it is much closer now than it was in 1831.

Although intertwined, there is a difference between "the signs of the times" and the "appearances of the Savior." We will point out many signs signaling that the Second Coming is rapidly approaching. We will outline the four categories of appearances which culminate in the Savior's coming in the clouds of heaven.

The *first appearance* of the Savior leading up to His appearance to the world is happening now. "The Lord who shall suddenly *come to his temple*" (D&C 133:2, emphasis added; see also D&C 36:8). The Lord promised:

> And inasmuch as my people build a house unto me in the name of the Lord, and do not suffer any unclean thing to come into it, that it be not defiled, my glory shall rest upon it;
>
> Yea, and my presence shall be there, for I will come into it, and all the pure in heart that shall come into it shall see God. (D&C 97:15–16)

These special appearances are not the experiences that would be broadcast on prime-time television or reported in the newspaper. This promise will also have a greater fulfillment in a future temple at Jackson County, Missouri. Each temple has an inscription over the door: "Holiness to the LORD—House of the Lord." Why would we be surprised that He has and will continue to visit His own houses?

As far as world conditions preceding the Second Coming, if you watch or listen to the daily news, these two verses could come from any news cast:

> And in that day shall be heard of wars and rumors of wars, and the whole earth shall be in commotion, and men's hearts shall fail them, and they shall say that Christ delayeth his coming until the end of the earth. [The end of the earth is at the end of the Millennium—see D&C 88:101. The end of the world, which is described as wickedness, is at the Second Coming—see Joseph Smith—Matthew 1:4]

And the love of men shall wax cold, and iniquity shall abound. (D&C 45:26–27)

Continuing in that section, the Lord reveals:

> And in that generation shall the times of the Gentiles be fulfilled. [Note: When the Lord used that term "in that generation" in verse 21 it was 36 years after the prophecy was given when it was fulfilled.]
>
> And there shall be men standing in that generation, that shall not pass until they shall see an overflowing scourge; for a desolating sickness shall cover the land.
>
> But my disciples shall stand in holy places, and shall not be moved; but among the wicked, men shall lift up their voices and curse God and die.
>
> And there shall be earthquakes also in divers places, and many desolations; yet men will harden their hearts against me, and they will take up the sword, one against another, and they will kill one another. (D&C 45:30–33)

A careful reading of Doctrine and Covenants section 45 will reveal that, from verse 16 to 59 (except verse 34), the Lord was repeating what He had told His disciples in 34 A.D. when they asked about His Second Coming, which is recorded in Matthew 24. Joseph Smith re-translated that chapter, and it is found in Joseph Smith—Matthew in the Pearl of Great Price.

The Lord continues to explain the signs that will precede His coming:

> Even so it shall be in that day when they shall see all these things, then shall they know that the hour is nigh.
>
> And it shall come to pass that he that feareth me shall be looking forth for the great day of the Lord to come, even for the signs of the coming of the Son of Man.
>
> And they shall see signs and wonders, for they shall be shown forth in the heavens above, and in the earth beneath.

> And they shall behold blood, and fire, and vapors of smoke.
>
> And before the day of the Lord shall come, the sun shall be darkened, and the moon be turned into blood, and the stars fall from heaven.
>
> And the remnant shall be gathered unto this place;
>
> And then they shall look for me, and, behold, I will come; and they shall see me in the clouds of heaven, clothed with power and great glory; with all the holy angels; and he that watches not for me shall be cut off. (D&C 45:38–44)

Before that appearance when He comes in the clouds of heaven, the wicked will see more sorrow and suffering than we can imagine. Here is just a sampling of what the Lord said in Doctrine and Covenants section 29:

> For the hour is nigh and the day soon at hand when the earth is ripe; and all the proud and they that do wickedly shall be as stubble; and I will burn them up, saith the Lord of Hosts, that wickedness shall not be upon the earth;
>
> For the hour is nigh, and that which was spoken by mine apostles must be fulfilled; for as they spoke so shall it come to pass;
>
> For I will reveal myself from heaven with power and great glory, with all the hosts thereof, and dwell in righteousness with men on earth a thousand years, and the wicked shall not stand.
>
> . . . But, behold, I say unto you that before this great day shall come the sun shall be darkened, and the moon shall be turned into blood, and the stars shall fall from heaven, and there shall be greater signs in heaven above and in the earth beneath;
>
> And there shall be weeping and wailing among the hosts of men;

> And there shall be a great hailstorm sent forth to destroy the crops of the earth.
>
> And it shall come to pass, because of the wickedness of the world, that I will take *vengeance upon the wicked*, for they will not repent; for the cup of mine indignation is full; for behold, my blood shall not cleanse them if they hear me not.
>
> Wherefore, I the Lord God will send forth flies upon the face of the earth, which shall take hold of the inhabitants thereof, and shall eat their flesh, and shall cause maggots to come in upon them;
>
> And their tongues shall be stayed that they shall not utter against me; and their flesh shall fall from off their bones, and their eyes from their sockets;
>
> And it shall come to pass that the beasts of the forest and the fowls of the air shall devour them up.
>
> And the great and abominable church, which is the whore of all the earth, shall be cast down by devouring fire, according as it is spoken by the mouth of Ezekiel the prophet, who spoke of these things, which have not come to pass but surely must, as I live, for abominations shall not reign. (D&C 29:9–11, 14–21, emphasis added).

That is a frightening prophecy but note that the vengeance is upon the wicked—not the righteous. Those verses seem to describe mass, unburied dead. You should also be aware that one of the Lord's definitions of "abominations" is found in Leviticus 18:22—it describes homosexuality!

The first categories of appearances preceding the Second Coming will be to His Saints in the various temples around the world. Now we need to have a history lesson as we introduce the next appearance of the Savior.

In Doctrine and Covenants 107:53–56, the Lord revealed:

> Three years previous to the death of Adam, he called Seth, Enos, Cainan, Mahalaleel, Jared, Enoch, and Methuselah, who were all high priests, with the residue of his posterity who were righteous, into the valley of Adam-ondi-Ahman, and there bestowed upon them his last blessing.
>
> And the Lord appeared unto them, and they rose up and blessed Adam, and called him Michael, the prince, the archangel.
>
> And the Lord administered comfort unto Adam, and said unto him: I have set thee to be at the head; a multitude of nations shall come of thee, and thou art a prince over them forever.
>
> And Adam stood up in the midst of the congregation; and, notwithstanding he was bowed down with age, being full of the Holy Ghost, predicted whatsoever should befall his posterity unto the latest generation.

It had been 927 years since Adam and Eve were barred from the Garden of Eden. Adam knew his time in mortality was coming to an end and wanted to hold one more "General Conference." During that event, Adam is shown in vision everything that would happen on the earth to the end of time. Enoch recorded it (see D&C 107:57). The pre-mortal Savior appeared and explained to Adam that he would preside over another meeting at Adam-ondi-Ahman before the Second Coming (see D&C 116).

You may want to research more concerning that meeting. The Old Testament prophet Daniel described it in Daniel 7. It is beyond the scope of this book to go into detail about that meeting other than to say that all those who have held keys of the priesthood, from deacon quorum presidents to the presidents of the Church, will be asked to report their stewardships. Undoubtedly there will be many meetings to prepare for the Second Coming—including Relief Society meetings, priesthood meetings, sacrament meetings, and administrative meetings. It certainly is something to look forward to. The Savior will be there to greet His faithful saints from all generations.

The *second category of appearances will be at Adam-ondi-Ahman* in the state of Missouri.

The *third appearance will be to the Jews in Jerusalem.* The conditions leading up to this appearance are scattered throughout the scriptures. Perhaps a simple outline is the best way to cover the events associated with this appearance:

1. Joseph Smith—Matthew 1:12—The first "abomination of desolation." We already described that one, it took place in 70 A.D.
2. The second "abomination of desolation" is mentioned in Joseph Smith—Matthew 1:32–34. This will all happen within "the generation" when the Savior shall come.
3. Joel 2:3—"A fire devoureth before them; and behind them a flame burneth: the land is as the garden of Eden before them, and behind them a desolate wilderness; yea, and nothing shall escape them."
4. An army of 200 million will siege Jerusalem (Revelation 9:16).
5. They will not destroy city for 42 months (i.e. 3½ years). Read about the two prophets who will protect the Jews from the army mentioned in #4 above. (Revelation 11)
6. Half the city will be destroyed—men killed, women ravished, children's heads dashed against the rocks (Zechariah 14:2–8).
7. Jews will flee across Kedron Valley to the Mount of Olives for possible escape.
8. The Savior and 144,000 men (Revelation 14:1) will appear just in time to save them from total annihilation. Brethren, how would you like to be part of that chosen group? Scriptural prerequisites

are found in Revelation 14: 3–4—they are redeemed and have not defiled themselves with women. A blessing certainly worth living for.

9. Doctrine and Covenants 45:51–53 gives an account of the Jews' conversion after the destruction of the massive army.
10. Ezekiel 39:9–12—It will require seven months to bury the dead; and for seven years the Jews will burn implements of war for heat.

It should be obvious that many details have been left out of this outline and that it will require a lot of study on your part to fill in the blanks. Again, the caution—do not try to teach everything you think you know. It will overwhelm your investigators and members who are not founded in the scriptures.

There are many cataclysmic events that will happen on earth preceding the Second Coming of the Lord in the clouds of heaven. One more scriptural account should cement in your mind that the Lord has given us a lot of information to prepare us if we would take the time to study and learn it.

> For behold, the Lord God hath sent forth the angel crying through the midst of heaven, saying: Prepare ye the way of the Lord, and make his paths straight, for the hour of his coming is nigh—
>
> When the Lamb shall stand upon Mount Zion, and with him a hundred and forty-four thousand, having his Father's name written on their foreheads.
>
> Wherefore, prepare ye for the coming of the Bridegroom; go ye, go ye out to meet him.
>
> For behold, he shall stand upon the mount of Olivet, and upon the mighty ocean, even the great deep, and upon the islands of the sea, and upon the land of Zion.
>
> And he shall utter his voice out of Zion, and he shall speak from Jerusalem, and his voice shall be heard among all people;

And it shall be a voice as the voice of many waters, and as the voice of a great thunder, which shall break down the mountains, and the valleys shall not be found.

He shall command the great deep, and it shall be driven back into the north countries, and the islands shall become one land;

And the land of Jerusalem and the land of Zion shall be turned back into their own place, and the earth shall be like as it was in the days before it was divided.

And the Lord, even the Savior, shall stand in the midst of his people, and shall reign over all flesh.

And they who are in the north countries shall come in remembrance before the Lord; and their prophets shall hear his voice, and shall no longer stay themselves; and they shall smite the rocks, and the ice shall flow down at their presence.

And an highway shall be cast up in the midst of the great deep.

Their enemies shall become a prey unto them,

And in the barren deserts there shall come forth pools of living water; and the parched ground shall no longer be a thirsty land.

And they shall bring forth their rich treasures unto the children of Ephraim, my servants.

And the boundaries of the everlasting hills shall tremble at their presence.

And there shall they fall down and be crowned with glory, even in Zion, by the hands of the servants of the Lord, even the children of Ephraim.

And they shall be filled with songs of everlasting joy.

> Behold, this is the blessing of the everlasting God upon the tribes of Israel, and the richer blessing upon the head of Ephraim and his fellows. (D&C 133:17–34)

Each sign could be enlarged and expanded upon for your understanding. However, only a small fraction of the revealed signs have been listed in this chapter. Hopefully, this will whet your appetite to put aside fun and games and become schooled in things that have eternal significance.

The *fourth and final appearance of the Savior* is an event that is difficult to envision. It is *to the entire world.* The actual description may cause you to alter what is commonly taught—even by some Church members.

> And it shall be answered upon their heads; for the presence of the Lord shall be as the melting fire that burneth, and as the fire which causeth the waters to boil. . . .
>
> And it shall be said: Who is this that cometh down from God in heaven with *dyed garments*; yea, from the regions which are not known, clothed in his glorious apparel, traveling in the greatness of his strength?
>
> And he shall say: I am he who spake in righteousness, mighty to save.
>
> And the Lord shall *be red in his apparel*, and his garments like him that treadeth in the wine–vat.
>
> And so great shall be the glory of his presence that the sun shall hide his face in shame, and the moon shall withhold its light, and the stars shall be hurled from their places.
>
> And his voice shall be heard: I have trodden the wine–press alone, and have brought judgment upon all people; and none were with me;
>
> And I have trampled them in my fury, and I did tread upon them in mine anger, and *their blood have I sprinkled upon my garments, and stained all my raiment*; for this

> was the day of vengeance which was in my heart. (D&C 133:41, 46–51, emphasis added).

For your investigators:

It is tempting to set aside all other doctrine and principles and focus solely upon the Second Coming. However, that would be a grave mistake. You are called to cry repentance to the people. That doesn't mean you don't talk of other doctrine but everything you teach should motivate your investigators to repent and come unto Christ.

As you study the scriptures, make note of the hundreds of signs given to alert the Saints of the approaching Second Coming. Then go on about your missionary work and your life, living as though the Second Coming would arrive tomorrow. Indeed, the Savior said it would:

> Behold, now *it is called today until the coming of the Son of Man,* and verily it is a day of sacrifice, and a day for the tithing of my people; for he that is tithed shall not be burned at his coming.
>
> *For after today cometh the burning*—this is speaking after the manner of the Lord—for verily I say, tomorrow all the proud and they that do wickedly shall be as stubble; and I will burn them up, for I am the Lord of Hosts; and I will not spare any that remain in Babylon.
>
> Wherefore, if ye believe me, ye will labor while it is called today. (D&C 64:23–25)

Chapter 22

Marriage and Children

You are entering a world that has been turned upside down by judges and lawmakers who have chosen to openly defy God's commandments. Know for sure that no amount of legislation or judicial decisions or public opinion can alter the revealed word of God. Also realize that you will meet people who will aggressively promote alternate lifestyles and practices which are contrary to God's commandments. Do not argue with them. Simply teach the truth, bear your testimony, and leave. Your job it not to convert—that belongs to the Holy Ghost. Your job is to teach the pure gospel in such a plain, powerful, straightforward way that people cannot misunderstand.

Realize that eternal marriage between a man and a woman, sealed in the temple, is prerequisite to gaining exaltation. The Church has been charged and empowered by God to perform ordinances necessary to open the gates to the highest degree of the celestial kingdom. For the Church to approve of same-sex marriages would be in total opposition to our God-given charge.

No matter how persuasive the argument or seemingly logical the discussion legitimizing same-sex marriage, you are sent forth to defend the God-revealed doctrine that marriage is between a man and a woman.

When God created Adam, he was surrounded by animals, birds, fishes and all the beauties of nature. However, He who knows all things said it was not good for man to be alone. He therefore created Eve and brought her to Adam. From that point on he is referred to as "the man and his wife."

> And the Lord God said, It is not good that the man should be alone; I will make him an help meet for him.
>
> And out of the ground the Lord God formed every beast of the field, and every fowl of the air; and brought them unto Adam to see what he would call them: and whatsoever Adam called every living creature, that was the name thereof.
>
> And Adam gave names to all cattle, and to the fowl of the air, and to every beast of the field; but for Adam there was not found an help meet for him.
>
> And the Lord God caused a deep sleep to fall upon Adam, and he slept: and he took one of his ribs, and closed up the flesh instead thereof;
>
> And the rib, which the Lord God had taken from man, made he a woman, and brought her unto the man.
>
> And Adam said, This is now bone of my bones, and flesh of my flesh: she shall be called Woman, because she was taken out of Man.
>
> Therefore shall a man leave his father and his mother, and shall cleave unto *his wife*: and they shall be one flesh.
>
> And they were both naked, *the man and his wife*, and were not ashamed. (Genesis 2:18–25, emphasis added)

In our day, the Lord included in His law to the Church: "Thou shalt love thy wife with all thy heart, and shalt cleave unto her and none else" (D&C 42:22).

When the Lord sent missionaries to the "Shaking Quakers" (D&C 49), the following information was revealed to correct their mistaken doctrine:

> And again, verily I say unto you, that whoso forbiddeth to marry is not ordained of God, for marriage is ordained of God unto man.
>
> Wherefore, it is lawful that he should have one wife, and they twain shall be one flesh, and all this that the earth might answer the end of its creation;
>
> And that it might be filled with the measure of man, according to his creation before the world was made. (D&C 49:15–17)

Given the number of failed marriages (both in the world and in the Church), it is imperative that you be a strong, unwavering voice for marriage. The institution of marriage is good and can result in the happiest of all conditions *if* the couple will follow the prophetic counsel and scriptural admonitions. The Lord commanded: "Thou shalt live together in love" (D&C 42:45), if that is not possible, the Lord would not command it.

Although you may be young and unmarried, you are still the Lord's ambassadors to take His truths to the darkening world. If you come from a broken home, without condemning your parents, identify what they did wrong and then teach people how to be successful.

Realize that Satan's greatest efforts will be to destroy marriages and families. Even temple marriages require great effort and sacrifices to ensure that they will be together in the eternal world.

In Doctrine and Covenants 132:7, the Lord revealed that three things must happen to all ordinances before they are valid in the eternities:

1. They must be "made."
2. They must be "entered into."
3. They must be "sealed by the Holy Spirit of promise."

"Making" the covenant is a single act observable by all who are watching. For baptism that means standing in the water, being immersed in the water, and coming out of the water. For eternal marriage that means kneeling across the altar from each other and responding to the question of taking the spouse as husband or wife. That is the easy part.

"Entering into" the covenant means living by the promises you "made" at the time the covenant was made. For baptism that means you:

> . . . are willing to bear one another's burdens, that they may be light;
>
> Yea, and are willing to mourn with those that mourn; yea, and comfort those that stand in need of comfort, and to stand as witnesses of God at all times and in all things, and in all places that ye may be in, even until death. (Mosiah 18:8–9)

For Eternal Marriage it means treating each other as you envision our Heavenly Parents treating each other.

Of course, no one is perfect, and we all make mistakes. However, the presence of the Holy Spirit in your marriage signifies that you are living as well as the Lord expects given the amount of light and knowledge He has given you. As long as that Spirit is there, you are heading in the right direction, and, if you continue, will eventually receive eternal life.

If the Spirit withdraws from your marriage, that is Heavenly Father's way of alerting you that you are not keeping your covenant and your eternal marriage is in jeopardy. It is also the way that Heavenly Father nudges you to fine tune and improve upon your relationship as you move to become more god-like.

As long as that Spirit is in your marriage, you have the promise that you will eventually receive eternal life. So, the temporary "seal of the Holy Spirit of promise" becomes permanent as you daily "enter into" the covenants you have made. Read Doctrine and Covenants 132:19–25 for an in depth description of the blessings that come from temple marriage.

You may encounter people who claim that their minister said the words, "I marry you for time and all eternity," supposing that merely saying the words will insure that their marriage will be valid in the eternal worlds. However, the Lord revealed:

> And again, verily I say unto you, if a man marry a wife, and make a covenant with her for time and for all eternity, if that covenant is not by me or by my word, which is my law, and is not sealed by the Holy Spirit of promise, through him whom I have anointed and appointed unto this power, then it is not valid neither of force when they are out of the world, because they are not joined by me, saith the Lord, neither by my word; when they are out of the world it cannot be received there, because the angels and the gods are appointed there, by whom they cannot pass; they cannot, therefore, inherit my glory; for my house is a house of order, saith the Lord God. (D&C 132:18)

Not only are those barred from entering the celestial kingdom by angels because they do not know the key words to pass successfully by them, but this also bars those who were married in the temple but have failed to "enter into" their temple covenants. The seal of the Holy Spirit of promise may be invisible to mortal eyes, but those guardian angels that we must pass can readily discern who has the seal and who does not.

Another group the Lord identifies are those who marry for time only but claim that God will not keep them apart merely because they didn't marry in the temple. Of this group, the Lord revealed:

> Therefore, if a man marry him a wife in the world, and he marry her not by me nor by my word, and he covenant with her so long as he is in the world and she with him, their covenant and marriage are not of force when they are dead, and when they are out of the world; therefore, they are not bound by any law when they are out of the world.
>
> Therefore, when they are out of the world they neither marry nor are given in marriage; but are appointed angels in heaven, which angels are ministering servants, to minister for those who are worthy of a far more, and an exceeding, and an eternal weight of glory.
>
> For these angels did not abide my law; therefore, they cannot be enlarged, but remain separately and singly,

> without exaltation, in their saved condition, to all eternity; and from henceforth are not gods, but are angels of God forever and ever. (D&C 132:15–17)

Many times during my years of teaching, I have been confronted with the statement that the Lord would not prevent them from being together forever by couples trying to justify not marrying in the temple. I readily agree—to their amazement. Then I say, "The Lord won't keep you apart—*you* will! If you fail to take advantage of the key (temple marriage) God has made available to you, don't accuse Him for your inability to unlock the gate to the highest degree of the celestial kingdom."

Those referred to in verses 14–17 actually sign their bill of divorcement at the time they are married. They only lay claim to each other "until death do us part" or "so long as we both shall live." As described in those verses, they will live "separately and singly, without exaltation, in their saved condition, to all eternity." What a sobering thought considering the eternal consequences for not accepting eternal marriage when it is offered to them.

The very purpose for marrying is to have children. Of course, some couples cannot have children—the Lord will reward their desire as though they had children. Eventually, in eternity, they will be blessed with children. Couples who marry merely to legitimize intimate relationships have missed the mark.

Children are intended to be not only the blessing of marriage but also provide a vital part of gaining the experience of parenting. Parenting is a major part of what exalted people will be doing in eternity. Mortal parenting is like a pre-run where couples gain valuable experience and learn vital lessons.

The Lord outlines the responsibilities of parents toward children in Doctrine and Covenants 68:25–32:

> And again, inasmuch as parents have children in Zion, or in any of her stakes which are organized, that teach them not to understand the doctrine of repentance, faith in Christ the Son of the living God, and of baptism and the gift of the Holy Ghost by the laying on of the hands, when eight years old, the sin be upon the heads of the parents.

> For this shall be a law unto the inhabitants of Zion, or in any of her stakes which are organized.
>
> And their children shall be baptized for the remission of their sins when eight years old, and receive the laying on of the hands.
>
> And they shall also teach their children to pray, and to walk uprightly before the Lord.
>
> And the inhabitants of Zion shall also observe the Sabbath day to keep it holy.
>
> And the inhabitants of Zion also shall remember their labors, inasmuch as they are appointed to labor, in all faithfulness; for the idler shall be had in remembrance before the Lord.
>
> Now, I, the Lord, am not well pleased with the inhabitants of Zion, for there are idlers among them; and their children are also growing up in wickedness; they also seek not earnestly the riches of eternity, but their eyes are full of greediness.
>
> These things ought not to be, and must be done away from among them.

As you teach investigators and interface with members of the Church, you will see gross violations of parental responsibilities. Make sure you teach them with gentleness, with the Spirit, and with love—leave their judgment to God.

If you are a young, single missionary, you are teaching principles, doctrines, and theories but you will have had no personal experience at parenting. Be particularly careful not to teach the ever-shifting philosophies of men. During the lifetime of the author, parenting philosophies have shifted from total indulgence without any correction, to physical punishment for the slightest wrong, back to permissiveness, and anywhere in between. Teach what the Lord has revealed in the scriptures and through living prophets and encourage them to prayerfully ask for inspiration on how to raise and discipline their children.

Remind them that they are being allowed to practice their parenting skills on Heavenly Father's children. Therefore, familiarize yourself with "The Family—a Proclamation to the World" and use that as a standard for marital relations and family practices.

The Family—A Proclamation to the World

> We, the First Presidency and the Council of the Twelve Apostles of The Church of Jesus Christ of Latter-day Saints, solemnly proclaim that marriage between a man and a woman is ordained of God and that the family is central to the Creator's plan for the eternal destiny of His children.
>
> All human beings—male and female—are created in the image of God. Each is a beloved spirit son or daughter of heavenly parents, and, as such, each has a divine nature and destiny. Gender is an essential characteristic of individual premortal, mortal, and eternal identity and purpose.
>
> In the premortal realm, spirit sons and daughters knew and worshipped God as their Eternal Father and accepted His plan by which His children could obtain a physical body and gain earthly experience to progress toward perfection and ultimately realize his or her divine destiny as heirs of eternal life. The divine plan of happiness enables family relationships to be perpetuated beyond the grave. Sacred ordinances and covenants available in holy temples make it possible for individuals to return to the presence of God and for families to be united eternally.
>
> The first commandment that God gave to Adam and Eve pertained to their potential for parenthood as husband and wife. We declare that God's commandment for His children to multiply and replenish the earth remains in force. We further declare that God has commanded that the sacred powers of procreation are to be employed only between man and woman, lawfully wedded as husband and wife.

We declare the means by which mortal life is created to be divinely appointed. We affirm the sanctity of life and of its importance in God's eternal plan.

Husband and wife have a solemn responsibility to love and care for each other and for their children. "Children are an heritage of the Lord" (Psalm 127:3). Parents have a sacred duty to rear their children in love and righteousness, to provide for their physical and spiritual needs, and to teach them to love and serve one another, observe the commandments of God and to be law-abiding citizens wherever they live. Husbands and wives—mothers and fathers— will be held accountable before God for the discharge of these obligations.

The family is ordained of God. Marriage between man and woman is essential to His eternal plan. Children are entitled to birth within the bonds of matrimony, and to be reared by a father and a mother who honor marital vows with complete fidelity. Happiness in family life is most likely to be achieved when founded upon the teachings of the Lord Jesus Christ. Successful marriages and families are established and maintained on principles of faith, prayer, repentance, forgiveness, respect, love, compassion, work, and wholesome recreational activities. By divine design, fathers are to preside over their families in love and righteousness and are responsible to provide the necessities of life and protection for their families. Mothers are primarily responsible for the nurture of their children. In these sacred responsibilities, fathers and mothers are obligated to help one another as equal partners. Disability, death, or other circumstances may necessitate individual adaptation. Extended families should lend support when needed.

We warn that individuals who violate covenants of chastity, who abuse spouse or offspring, or who fail to fulfill family responsibilities will one day stand accountable before God.

> Further, we warn that the disintegration of the family will bring upon individuals, communities, and nations the calamities foretold by ancient and modern prophets.
>
> We call upon responsible citizens and officers of government everywhere to promote those measures designed to maintain and strengthen the family as the fundamental unit of society. ("The Family: A Proclamation to the World," *Ensign*, Nov. 2010, 129)

This document is not only revelatory but is accepted as the mind and will of the Lord in our day. One cannot read this document without believing that prophets, seers, and revelators were shown by the Lord what conditions would exist in our day and what remedies to offset Satan's destructive efforts.

For your investigators:

This entire chapter is something that can and should be taught to those who are nearing baptism. Be careful not to teach too much too fast. It will require the spirit of the Holy Ghost in their lives to enlighten their understanding and confirm to their souls that which you are teaching but have not, as yet, lived yourselves.

Chapter 23

The Millennium

As world conditions continue to deteriorate, the approach of the Millennium becomes even more desirable. What initiates the Millennium? The Second Coming of the Lord. Leading up to that day will be a total meltdown of morals and civility among the wicked. The Lord said: "But as it was in the days of Noah, so it shall be also at the coming of the Son of Man" (Joseph Smith—Matthew 1:41).

How was it in the days of Noah?

> And God saw that the wickedness of men had become great in the earth; and every man was lifted up in the imagination of the thoughts of his heart, being only evil continually. . . .
>
> And God said unto Noah: The end of all flesh is come before me, for the earth is filled with violence, and behold I will destroy all flesh from off the earth. (Moses 8:22, 30)

How close are we to those two conditions—thoughts evil continually, and the earth is full of violence? One cannot say with exactness, but the Lord said:

> Behold, the day has come, when the cup of the wrath of mine indignation is full.

> Behold, verily I say unto you, that these are the words of the Lord your God.
>
> Wherefore, labor ye, labor ye in my vineyard for the last time—for the last time call upon the inhabitants of the earth.
>
> For in mine own due time will I come upon the earth in judgment, and my people shall be redeemed and shall reign with me on earth.
>
> For the great Millennium, of which I have spoken by the mouth of my servants, shall come.
>
> For Satan shall be bound, and when he is loosed again he shall only reign for a little season, and then cometh the end of the earth. (D&C 43:26–31)

For those who are alive when the Second Coming happens, the Lord said: "And the saints that are upon the earth, who are alive, shall be quickened and be caught up to meet him" (D&C 88:96).

Your Christian investigators will call this "the rapture," although that term is never used in the Bible.

One of the most desirable conditions during the Millennium is described in Doctrine and Covenants 45:58–59, where the Lord revealed:

> And the earth shall be given unto them for an inheritance; and they shall multiply and wax strong, and their children shall grow up without sin unto salvation.
>
> For the Lord shall be in their midst, and his glory shall be upon them, and he will be their king and their lawgiver.

Satan will be bound during the Millennium. How will that happen? There are at least three ways:

1. The destruction of the wicked. "For behold, saith the prophet, the time cometh speedily that Satan shall have no more power over the hearts of the children of men; for the day soon cometh that all the proud and they who do wickedly shall be as

stubble; and the day cometh that they must be burned" (1 Nephi 22:15).

2. The righteousness of those who are not destroyed at the Second Coming. "And because of the righteousness of his people, Satan has no power; wherefore, he cannot be loosed for the space of many years; for he hath no power over the hearts of the people, for they dwell in righteousness, and the Holy One of Israel reigneth" (1 Nephi 22:26).
3. By the power of God. "Satan shall be bound, that old serpent, who is called the devil, and shall not be loosed for the space of a thousand years" (D&C 88:110).

Will Satan ever have power over the people again? Yes. The Lord said at the conclusion of the thousand years: "And again, verily, verily, I say unto you that when the thousand years are ended, and men again begin to deny their God, then will I spare the earth but for a little season" (D&C 29:22).

To complete the revealed doctrine about what will happen when Satan is loosed again, the Lord revealed:

> . . . Satan shall be bound, that old serpent, who is called the devil, and shall not be loosed for the space of a thousand years.
>
> And then he shall be loosed for a little season, that he may gather together his armies.
>
> And Michael, the seventh angel, even the archangel, shall gather together his armies, even the hosts of heaven.
>
> And the devil shall gather together his armies; even the hosts of hell, and shall come up to battle against Michael and his armies.
>
> And then cometh the battle of the great God; and the devil and his armies shall be cast away into their own place, that they shall not have power over the saints any more at all.

> For Michael shall fight their battles, and shall overcome him who seeketh the throne of him who sitteth upon the throne, even the Lamb. (D&C 88:110–115)

We mention this here because it is the extension of what will happen following the Millennium. It is difficult to envision why people will turn away from the Savior, who will be in their very midst, and, through their unrighteousness, allow Satan to be loosed from his prison house. That, however, is the Lord's prophecy and it will be fulfilled.

Of greatest appeal is that the Savior will dwell with people during the Millennium. He said: "For I will reveal myself from heaven with power and great glory, with all the hosts thereof, and dwell in righteousness with men on earth a thousand years, and the wicked shall not stand" (D&C 29:11).

Joseph Smith clarified this statement:

> . . . Christ and the resurrected Saints will reign over the earth during the thousand years. They will not probably dwell upon the earth, but will visit it when they please, or when it is necessary to govern it. (*History of the Church*, 5:212*)*

The description of the Millennium is something wonderful to contemplate. After describing the resurrection of those who die before the beginning of the Millennium, the Lord says:

> And he that liveth when the Lord shall come, and hath kept the faith, blessed is he; nevertheless, it is appointed to him to die at the age of man.
>
> Wherefore, children shall grow up until they become old; old men shall die; but they shall not sleep in the dust, but they shall be changed in the twinkling of an eye. (D&C 63:50–51)

Visiting that same subject in more detail, the Lord revealed:

Behold, it is my will, that all they who call on my name, and worship me according to mine everlasting gospel, should gather together, and stand in holy places;

And prepare for the revelation which is to come, when the veil of the covering of my temple, in my tabernacle, which hideth the earth, shall be taken off, and all flesh shall see me together.

And every corruptible thing, both of man, or of the beasts of the field, or of the fowls of the heavens, or of the fish of the sea, that dwells upon all the face of the earth, shall be consumed;

And also that of element shall melt with fervent heat; and all things shall become new, that my knowledge and glory may dwell upon all the earth.

And in that day the enmity of man, and the enmity of beasts, yea, the enmity of all flesh, shall cease from before my face.

And in that day whatsoever any man shall ask, it shall be given unto him.

And in that day Satan shall not have power to tempt any man.

And there shall be no sorrow because there is no death.

In that day an infant shall not die until he is old; and his life shall be as the age of a tree;

And when he dies he shall not sleep, that is to say in the earth, but shall be changed in the twinkling of an eye, and shall be caught up, and his rest shall be glorious.

Yea, verily I say unto you, in that day when the Lord shall come, he shall reveal all things—

Things which have passed, and hidden things which no man knew, things of the earth, by which it was made, and the purpose and the end thereof—

> Things most precious, things that are above, and things that are beneath, things that are in the earth, and upon the earth, and in heaven.
>
> And all they who suffer persecution for my name, and endure in faith, though they are called to lay down their lives for my sake yet shall they partake of all this glory
>
> Wherefore, fear not even unto death; for in this world your joy is not full, but in me your joy is full. (D&C 101:22–36)

The destruction at the Second Coming will be so intense that "every corruptible thing" will be destroyed. Also, the very elements of the earth will "melt with fervent heat." For what purpose? All disease and corruption will be destroyed. The earth will be elevated from its present telestial status (where the Holy Ghost is our main contact with God), to a terrestrial state where the Savior is our source of contact with the Godhead.

When "enmity" [mutual hatred or ill will] will cease. Isaiah 11:6–9; 65:25 described that time when the lamb and the leopard will lie down together, the lion will eat straw like the ox, a child will play with wild animals and a child will not be hurt while playing with poisonous vipers.

The Millennium is also a time when we can ask anything we desire of the Lord and He will give it to us or reveal it to us. In addition to Satan having no power to tempt us, there will be no sickness or premature death.

People will live "to the age of a tree," which Isaiah 65:20 says (emphasis added): "There shall be no more thence an infant of days, nor an old man that hath not filled his days: for the child shall die an *hundred years old*; but the sinner being an hundred years old shall be accursed."

There are arguments, even among the Latter-day Saints, as to the age of the earth, how it was created and peopled, etc. The Lord clearly states that He will give us that information when He comes. It would be wisdom on your part to avoid speculating or participating in discussions where the Lord states we won't know until He comes.

From what is written, it seems that when a person reaches one hundred years, he will be "changed in the twinkling of an eye" from mortality to immortality. There will be no graves for the bodies of the dead, neither will cremation be necessary.

With no sickness, disease, or premature death, the population of the earth during the Millennium will likely eclipse anything we have seen to this point in earth's history.

The task we face as missionaries is to instill in people a desire to live well enough to be spared the cleansing fire at the Second Coming so we can qualify to live during the early days of the Millennium—if it happens to come within our lifetime.

Avoid speculating as to when it will begin—we are told that no man knows the day or the hour of the Second Coming. Also, as with all other doctrine, don't give your opinion as though it is the doctrine of the Church.

If you don't know the answer to questions you are asked, admit that you don't know the answer and then search the scriptures and the teachings of Latter-day prophets to see if the answers have been revealed. If no answer has been revealed, don't try to guess what the Lord would say. Enough has been revealed to satisfy any honest truth-seeker with the expectations that when the Lord comes, He will reveal all things.

For your investigators:

Similar caution is given here as with the chapter on the Second Coming. Don't get caught up in speculation. As you can tell from the references used in this chapter, you will know considerably more than those who are not Latter-day Saints or members who are not diligent in their study of the scriptures.

As you continue your scriptural study, you will add many more mind-boggling insights into Millennial conditions. Those given in this chapter should provide a framework upon which you can add more interesting facts. Just follow the promptings of the Spirit so that you don't give too much too fast.

Chapter 24

Work for the Dead

Among the many doctrines which separate us from other Christian churches is the revelation that ordinances necessary for salvation and exaltation can be performed in temples by living members of the Church for those who passed away without hearing or embracing the fullness of the restored gospel.

The one unmistakable verse in the Bible proving that the Saints in Christ's time were doing vicarious or proxy ordinances for departed people is 1 Corinthians 15:29: "Else what shall they do which are baptized for the dead, if the dead rise not at all? why are they then baptized for the dead?"

Even the greatest of Christian scholars admit that they have no explanation for this verse. As part of the restoration of the gospel, the whole concept of vicarious work for the dead completes an otherwise very selective gospel. When you question your investigators about what happens to those countless billions of people who were born, lived, and died without ever hearing the name of Christ, they either don't know, have never thought about it, or claim that they are all going to hell. Pretty harsh punishment by God for those who never had the opportunity to exercise their agency!

Paul, to the Hebrew Saints, made this comment: "God having provided some better thing for us, that they without us should not be made perfect" (Hebrews 11:40).

What key do we hold that without us those who have gone before cannot be made perfect? Remember, the Savior told Nicodemus that without baptism by water and the Spirit, no one could enter into the kingdom of God (John 3:3-5).

It is important for you to realize that we are the only church on the face of the earth that provides a way for *every* son or daughter of Adam and Eve's family to have the opportunity to accept or reject the gospel.

Peter clearly explained that teaching was going on in the spirit world and the purpose for it:

> For Christ also hath once suffered for sins, the just for the unjust, that he might bring us to God, being put to death in the flesh, but quickened by the Spirit:
>
> By which also he went and preached unto the spirits in prison;
>
> Which sometime were disobedient, when once the longsuffering of God waited in the days of Noah, while the ark was a preparing, wherein few, that is, eight souls were saved by water. (1 Peter 3:18–20)
>
> For for this cause was the gospel preached also to them that are dead, that they might be judged according to men in the flesh, but live according to God in the spirit. (1 Peter 4:6)

Combining Peter's teaching and Paul's explanation that vicarious or proxy work was being performed for the dead, coupled with the Savior's teaching that baptism was a prerequisite for all who would enter into the kingdom of God, we have clear biblical proof that the gospel was to be made available to all of Adam and Eve's family.

From the very earliest times of the Restoration, when Moroni appeared to Joseph Smith (see D&C 2), the principle of the hearts of the fathers turning to their children and the children to their fathers was revealed. That was in 1823. It wasn't until 1836 that Elijah appeared to Joseph Smith and Oliver Cowdery and revealed the keys enabling the work for the dead to be performed.

The last of the four recorded visions in the Kirtland Temple on that glorious Sunday (April 3, 1836) was the fulfillment of the ancient prophet Malachi's prophecy:

> After this vision had closed, another great and glorious vision burst upon us; for Elijah the prophet, who was taken to heaven without tasting death, stood before us, and said:
>
> Behold, the time has fully come, which was spoken of by the mouth of Malachi—testifying that he [Elijah] should be sent, before the great and dreadful day of the Lord come—
>
> To turn the hearts of the fathers to the children, and the children to the fathers, lest the whole earth be smitten with a curse—
>
> Therefore, the keys of this dispensation are committed into your hands; and by this ye may know that the great and dreadful day of the Lord is near, even at the doors. (D&C 110:13–16)

It was six and a half years later that Joseph Smith started to expand the Saint's understanding of baptism for the dead. Doctrine and Covenants sections 127 and 128 give added knowledge about the directions and procedures for performing acceptable baptisms for the dead. Then, it gives this sobering concept: "For we without them cannot be made perfect; neither can they without us be made perfect. Neither can they nor we be made perfect without those who have died in the gospel also" (D&C 128:18).

As with the other principles of the gospel, baptism for the dead was revealed "line upon line and precept upon precept" (see D&C 98:12).

Since this will be such a new and unheard of doctrine, make sure your investigators understand that performing the ordinances for the dead does not necessarily mean they will accept the gospel in the spirit world. Performing the ordinances here on earth only opens the door for them to progress in the spirit world if they accept the gospel and live according to revealed principles.

How are the dead able to learn about the gospel? Joseph F. Smith had a vision of the spirit world just days before he passed away in 1918. He wrote:

> I beheld that the faithful elders of this dispensation, when they depart from mortal life, continue their labors in the preaching of the gospel of repentance and redemption, through the sacrifice of the Only Begotten Son of God, among those who are in darkness and under the bondage of sin in the great world of the spirits of the dead. (D&C 138:57)

Then he clearly saw that the burden of accepting the gospel and acting upon it, rests with the dead. The vision continued:

> The dead who repent will be redeemed, through obedience to the ordinances of the house of God,
>
> And after they have paid the penalty of their transgressions, and are washed clean, shall receive a reward according to their works, for they are heirs of salvation. (D&C 138:58–59)

If the dead choose not to accept the gospel, and therefore do not repent, the proxy work done in their behalf would be the same as the fate of a person who was baptized but did not faithfully keep the covenants he had made. What is that fate? The Lord said:

> Hearken and hear, O ye my people, saith the Lord and your God, ye whom I delight to bless with the greatest of all blessings, ye that hear me; and ye that hear me not will I curse, that have professed my name, with the heaviest of all cursings. . . .
>
> He that receiveth my law and doeth it, the same is my disciple; and he that saith he receiveth it and doeth it not, the same is not my disciple, and shall be cast out from among you. (D&C 41:1, 5)

Some well-intended but ignorant investigators might suggest they will wait until they get to the spirit world and then accept the gospel and still gain eternal life. The likelihood of them joining and being faithful there when they turn their backs on it here, is not very good. It is like playing Russian Roulette with no blanks in the pistol.

It is important to realize that God never uses force to achieve His objective. The gospel is freely offered to every son and daughter of Adam and Eve, either while they are here on earth or in the spirit world. What if they heard it here but didn't accept it? Do they have a chance in the spirit world? Many Latter-day Saints would say they had their chance, and their fate was made sure. However, in Joseph F. Smith's vision he records:

> And as I wondered, my eyes were opened, and my understanding quickened, and I perceived that the Lord went not in person among the wicked and the disobedient who had rejected the truth, to teach them;
>
> But behold, from among the righteous, he organized his forces and appointed messengers, clothed with power and authority, and commissioned them to go forth and carry the light of the gospel to them that were in darkness, *even to all the spirits of men*; and thus was the gospel preached to the dead.
>
> And the chosen messengers went forth to declare the acceptable day of the Lord and proclaim liberty to the captives who were bound, even unto all who would repent of their sins and receive the gospel.
>
> Thus was the gospel preached to those who had died in their sins, *without a knowledge of the truth, or in transgression, having rejected the prophets.*
>
> These were taught faith in God, repentance from sin, vicarious baptism for the remission of sins, the gift of the Holy Ghost by the laying on of hands,
>
> And all other principles of the gospel that were necessary for them to know in order to qualify themselves that they might be judged according to men in the flesh, but

> live according to God in the spirit. (D&C 138:29–34, emphasis added).

Note the italicized words above. Even the wicked and disobedient who had rejected the truth were to be taught. We all readily agree that those who died without a knowledge of the truth would be given the opportunity to accept or reject the gospel, but the phrase "in transgression having rejected the prophets" often causes us to question if we have understood correctly the doctrine.

The key is to follow the Lord's command: "Leave judgment alone with me, for it is mine and I will repay. Peace be with you; my blessings continue with you" (D&C 82:23).

In other words, you and I don't have enough understanding of what conditions here on earth caused them to reject your message. We don't know if they had a "full chance" here or what the conditions are in the spirit world. Will it be easier to accept and live the gospel there than it is here? We don't know. If they had a full opportunity to accept the gospel here, will that determine whether they can still repent over there? Again, we don't know. We should do as the Lord suggests: Do their work. Find joy in your service. Enjoy the peace that comes from your righteous efforts and leave their judgment alone with God.

What were the wicked and disobedient taught? They were taught the first principles and ordinances of the gospel. But why teach them about baptism (the prerequisite for entering the celestial kingdom) if it were not possible for them to enter that kingdom?

Two verses quoted earlier shed light on what the repentant spirits must do to qualify for the celestial kingdom:

> The dead who repent will be redeemed, through obedience to the ordinances of the house of God,
>
> And after they have paid the penalty of their transgressions, and are washed clean, shall receive a reward according to their works, for they are heirs of salvation. (D&C 138:58–59)

First, we see that repentance is possible and necessary—even for the dead. Next, there seems to be a partial payment necessary for past sins. Presumably, that would be a payment for whatever portion of their sins they knew, understood, and willfully disobeyed while in mortality. Although "heirs of salvation" is used referring to those in the telestial kingdom (see D&C 76:88), the fact that those referred to in Joseph F. Smith's vision are "redeemed through obedience to the ordinances of the house of God" indicates that they can achieve the highest degree of the celestial kingdom. Remember, the ordinance of baptism is necessary for entrance into the celestial kingdom. The other ordinances of the temple are necessary only for entrance into the highest degree of the celestial kingdom.

For your investigators:

People often want to know what "Mormons" do in the temples for the dead. The simple answer is that we do the bare minimum necessary for them to gain exaltation. You should have cemented in your mind what those ordinances are: baptism, gift of the Holy Ghost, priesthood (for the brethren), endowment (including washing and anointing), and being sealed to a spouse in the temple. All five of those ordinances are performed in the temple for the dead.

You should be aware that children who die before the age of accountability are only required to be sealed to their parents. All other required ordinances are satisfied through the Atonement of Christ.

Chapter 25

Resurrection and Judgment

You must understand that the very first resurrection took place 2,000 years ago. Paul taught the Corinthian Saints: "But now is Christ risen from the dead, and become the firstfruits of them that slept" (1 Corinthians 15:20). No one from Adam to Christ had ever been resurrected. Some had been brought back to life, but they were destined to die at some future time.

At the Resurrection of Christ, many of those who had died before His crucifixion were resurrected. "And the graves were opened; and many bodies of the saints which slept arose, And came out of the graves after his resurrection, and went into the holy city, and appeared unto many" (Matthew 27:52–53).

However, following that first ever resurrection, we have record of only three people who died after Christ's Resurrection who have been resurrected (there may have been more but we have no official account of them): Peter, James, and Moroni—remember, John, the Beloved, was translated—not resurrected.

It appears that the first resurrection we will be permitted to participate in will be at the coming of Christ.

The best place to learn of the Resurrection is in Doctrine and Covenants section 88. Let's first take the timing of the Resurrection, then we'll discuss the criteria for each Resurrection.

In verse 96, the blessing of those who are alive at the Second Coming is outlined: "And the saints that are upon the earth, who are alive, shall be quickened and be caught up to meet him."

Verses 97–98 describe the resurrection of those who are going to the celestial kingdom. Although not mentioned by name in the scriptures, this is frequently referred to by latter-day prophets and in patriarchal blessings as "the morning of the first resurrection."

> And they who have slept in their graves shall come forth, for their graves shall be opened; and they also shall be caught up to meet him in the midst of the pillar of heaven—
>
> They are Christ's, the first fruits, they who shall descend with him first, and they who are on the earth and in their graves, who are first caught up to meet him; and all this by the voice of the sounding of the trump of the angel of God.

All celestial candidates who have died since the Resurrection of the Savior to His Second Coming will be resurrected and caught up to meet Him in the clouds. This Resurrection will apparently then continue throughout the Millennium as those living during that thousand year period will live to the age of a tree (see Isaiah 65:20 which explains that to be 100 years of age) and then be "changed in the twinkling of an eye" from mortality to immortality (see D&C 101:30–31).

Paul gave some clarification concerning the sequence of those who had died before the Second Coming and the "transfiguration"—or being caught up of those who are alive on the earth:

> For the Lord himself shall descend from heaven with a shout, with the voice of the archangel, and with the trump of God: and the dead in Christ shall rise first:
>
> Then we which are alive and remain shall be caught up together with them in the clouds, to meet the Lord in the air: and so shall we ever be with the Lord. (1 Thessalonians 4:16–17)

One can only imagine the joyous reunion of those who have died and those of their extended families who are alive on the earth. Early deaths, departed parents and siblings, friends who have passed away, and a host of others will all be there rejoicing as the Savior prepares to descend to the earth and usher in the Millennium. How long we will be in the clouds of heaven, is not specified. Knowing that the earth will be consumed by fire—every corruptible thing including the very elements—suggests we will have sufficient time to get reacquainted and catch up on what all of us have been doing. All your losses will be made up in that celestial resurrection.

Joseph Smith said:

> It is my meditation all the day, and more than my meat and drink, to know how I shall make the Saints of God comprehend the visions that roll like an overflowing surge before my mind. (*History of the Church*, 5:362)

> All your losses will be made up to you in the resurrection, provided you continue faithful. By the vision of the Almighty I have seen it. (*Teachings of the Prophet Joseph Smith*, 295)

The next part of the First Resurrection (often referred to by Church leaders as "the afternoon of the First Resurrection" or the Resurrection of the terrestrial people) is described in verse 99 and will begin sometime following the resurrection of the celestials. It will continue throughout the Millennium.

> And after this another angel shall sound, which is the second trump; and then cometh the redemption of those who are Christ's at his coming; who have received their part in that prison which is prepared for them, that they might receive the gospel, and be judged according to men in the flesh.

The resurrection of those going to the telestial kingdom is described in verses 100–101:

> And again, another trump shall sound, which is the third trump; and then come the spirits of men who are to be judged, and are found under condemnation;
>
> And these are the rest of the dead; and they live not again until the thousand years are ended, neither again, until the end of the earth.

These people will be held in spirit prison for 1,000 years, paying for their sins and learning as much as they can before their bodies are reunited with their spirits.

There is one more group who will follow the resurrection of the telestial people. They are the sons of perdition—those who had received bodies here on earth, embraced the gospel, and then allowed themselves to be overcome by the temptations of Satan. You will read more about these people in the final chapter of this book. They are mentioned in verse 102:

> And another trump shall sound, which is the fourth trump, saying: There are found among those who are to remain until that great and last day, even the end, who shall remain filthy still.

Every person born on this earth will be resurrected at some point in time. Paul stated it clearly: "For as in Adam all die, even so in Christ shall *all be made alive*. But every man in his own order: Christ the firstfruits; afterward they that are Christ's at his coming" (1 Corinthians 15:22–23, emphasis added).

Now we will see what the Lord has revealed concerning the qualifications for each of the Resurrections. Earlier in Section 88 starting in verse 15, the Lord explains that the spirit and the body constitute the soul of man. Then He states that the resurrection from the dead is the redemption of the soul.

It is worth noting that the very purpose of this earth is to become our celestial kingdom. The Lord revealed:

> And the redemption of the soul is through him that quickeneth all things, in whose bosom it is decreed that the poor and the meek of the earth shall inherit it.
>
> Therefore, it [the earth] must needs be sanctified from all unrighteousness, that it may be prepared for the celestial glory;
>
> For after it hath filled the measure of its creation, it shall be crowned with glory, even with the presence of God the Father;
>
> That bodies who are of the celestial kingdom may possess it forever and ever; for, for this intent was it [the earth] made and created, and for this intent are they sanctified. (D&C 88:17–20)

Further we learn another amazing fact:

> And again, verily I say unto you, the earth abideth the law of a celestial kingdom, for it filleth the measure of its creation, and transgresseth not the law—
>
> Wherefore, it shall be sanctified; yea, notwithstanding it shall die, it shall be quickened again, and shall abide the power by which it is quickened, and the righteous shall inherit it. (D&C 88:25–26)

Seldom do people view the earth as a free agent able to obey or disobey. However, this declaration about the earth "abiding the law of the celestial kingdom" and not transgressing the law would be meaningless unless the earth were capable of violating the law. Also, of interest is the fact that the earth is a living orb—or else how could it die?

In verses 20–24, the Lord explains that if a person is not sanctified through the "law of Christ"—which is the fullness of the gospel—all ordinances being activated by the Atonement of Christ—then they cannot inherit the celestial kingdom. These verses are so necessary for our understanding that we need to cite them here (emphasis added):

> That bodies who are of the celestial kingdom may possess it forever and ever; for, for this intent was it [the earth]

> made and created, and for this intent are they [people who join the Church] sanctified.
>
> And they who are not sanctified through the law which I have given unto you, even the law of Christ, must inherit another kingdom, even that of a terrestrial kingdom, or that of a telestial kingdom.
>
> For he who is not able to abide *the law* of a celestial kingdom cannot abide a celestial glory. [There should be no guess work who will go to the celestial kingdom. If a person is living the celestial law, they will go to the celestial kingdom. If they are not, they will not go there]
>
> And he who cannot abide *the law* of a terrestrial kingdom cannot abide a terrestrial glory.
>
> And he who cannot abide *the law* of a telestial kingdom cannot abide a telestial glory; therefore he is not meet for a kingdom of glory. Therefore he must abide a kingdom which is not a kingdom of glory.

However, it is evident in these verses that the level of law a person lives will determine which kingdom he or she inherits. However, any person who seriously evaluates the life he or she is living will come to the conclusion that they are not 100%. The Lord then takes that into account in verses 28–32: They who are of a celestial spirit shall receive the same body which was a natural body; even ye shall receive your bodies, and your glory shall be that glory by which your bodies are quickened.

> Ye who are quickened by a portion of the celestial glory shall then receive of the same, even a fulness.
>
> And they who are quickened by a portion of the terrestrial glory shall then receive of the same, even a fulness.
>
> And also they who are quickened by a portion of the telestial glory shall then receive of the same, even a fulness.
>
> And they who remain shall also be quickened; nevertheless, they shall return again to their own place, to enjoy that

> which they are willing to receive, because they were not willing to enjoy that which they might have received.

The "natural body" mentioned in verse 28 is one which has the power to procreate. No other resurrected bodies will have that power—only those in the highest degree of the celestial kingdom. But those "quickened by a portion" of the celestial spirit will be able to increase and grow until they receive a fullness. The same being said of those who are actuated by a portion of the terrestrial and telestial kingdoms.

However, the sons of perdition mentioned in verse 32 gives great insight into which kingdom we will be resurrected. Note that they will return to outer darkness "to enjoy" that which they were willing "to enjoy" because they were not willing "to enjoy" that which they might have received—which was the highest degree of the celestial kingdom.

Could we generalize and say that each person will be assigned to a kingdom where they will "enjoy" all they are willing to receive? Moroni further enlarges our understanding:

> Behold, I say unto you that ye would be more miserable to dwell with a holy and just God, under a consciousness of your filthiness before him, than ye would to dwell with the damned souls in hell. (Mormon 9:4)

It seems evident, therefore, that day by day we determine by our thoughts, words, and actions which kingdom we are preparing to enter at the day of judgment. It is naïve to believe we can live the telestial law—which is "eat, drink, and be merry" and do whatever you want to—and still inherit the celestial kingdom for our reward. That is also the message you must take to the world.

Judgment is something that strikes fear into the hearts of people—mostly because we don't understand it. For the righteous, the Lord says: "For thus saith the Lord, I will cut my work short in righteousness, for the days come that I will send forth judgment unto victory" (D&C 52:11).

The Savior described the judgment of the righteous by teaching: "Well done, good and faithful servant; thou hast been faithful over a few things, I will make thee ruler over many things: enter thou into the joy of thy lord" (Matthew 25:23). "Then shall the King say unto them on his right hand, Come, ye blessed of my Father, inherit the kingdom prepared for you from the foundation of the world" (Matthew 25:34).

Alma made this summary statement about factors that will be included in our final judgment:

> For our words will condemn us, yea, all our works will condemn us; we shall not be found spotless; and our thoughts will also condemn us; and in this awful state we shall not dare to look up to our God; and we would fain be glad if we could command the rocks and the mountains to fall upon us to hide us from his presence. (Alma 12:14)

Jacob, Nephi's brother, records this expansion to our understanding of judgment:

> Wherefore, we shall have a perfect knowledge of all our guilt, and our uncleanness, and our nakedness; and the righteous shall have a perfect knowledge of their enjoyment, and their righteousness, being clothed with purity, yea, even with the robe of righteousness.
>
> And it shall come to pass that when all men shall have passed from this first death unto life, insomuch as they have become immortal, they must appear before the judgment-seat of the Holy One of Israel; and then cometh the judgment, and then must they be judged according to the holy judgment of God.
>
> And assuredly, as the Lord liveth, for the Lord God hath spoken it, and it is his eternal word, which cannot pass away, that they who are righteous shall be righteous still, and they who are filthy shall be filthy still; wherefore, they who are filthy are the devil and his angels; and they shall go away into everlasting fire, prepared for them; and their torment is as a lake of fire and brimstone, whose flame ascendeth up forever and ever and has no end. (2 Nephi 9:14–16)

Moroni puts the capstone on resurrection and judgment when he wrote:

> And because of the redemption of man, which came by Jesus Christ, they are brought back into the presence of the Lord; yea, this is wherein all men are redeemed, because the death of Christ bringeth to pass the resurrection, which bringeth to pass a redemption from an endless sleep, from which sleep all men shall be awakened by the power of God when the trump shall sound; and they shall come forth, both small and great, and all shall stand before his bar, being redeemed and loosed from this eternal band of death, which death is a temporal death.
>
> And then cometh the judgment of the Holy One upon them; and then cometh the time that he that is filthy shall be filthy still; and he that is righteous shall be righteous still; he that is happy shall be happy still; and he that is unhappy shall be unhappy still. (Mormon 9:13–14)

Can you see the application of a principle taught by Joseph Smith as recorded in Doctrine and Covenants 130:20–21? "There is a law, irrevocably decreed in heaven before the foundations of this world, upon which all blessings are predicated—And when we obtain any blessing from God, it is by obedience to that law upon which it is predicated."

If we want to be happy, we must discover and live by the laws upon which happiness is predicated. If we want to earn a spot in the celestial kingdom, we must learn and live by the laws of the celestial kingdom. So, it is with every blessing we receive or hope to earn from God. There is no "something for nothing" principle in the day of judgment.

There are many times of partial judgment. For instance, every minute of every day we can live well enough to keep the Spirit with us—a constant partial judgment. So, the presence or absence of the Spirit can be viewed as an ongoing judgment. We are judged when we partake of the sacrament, when we attend tithing settlement, when we are interviewed for the priesthood or a church calling, when we renew our temple recommend, when we die, when we are resurrected, and then the final judgment at the end of the little season following the Millennium.

Judgment is not something to be feared but something we should be constantly preparing for.

For your investigators:

Much of your understanding of death and the spirit world (which is discussed in the following chapter) will bring comfort and hope to those who have lost loved ones. Be generous and quick in sharing your understanding with those who are grieving.

Although most Christians believe in a resurrection, few understand when it will happen, who will be involved, and the criteria which determines our position in the Resurrection. Many Christians do not believe in a literal resurrection of the body but believe in some mystical resurrection where we will be incorporated into the body of God.

Keep in mind the physical resurrection of Christ and assure your investigators that He is the role model for all of mankind.

You can do much to motivate your investigators as you explain judgment and how to prepare by watching our thoughts, words, and actions. To deny or ignore a final judgment does nothing to change the fact that it will happen. John, the Revelator, saw the final judgment and described it as follows:

> And I saw the dead, small and great, stand before God; and the books were opened: and another book was opened, which is the book of life: and the dead were judged out of those things which were written in the books, according to their works.
>
> And the sea gave up the dead which were in it; and death and hell delivered up the dead which were in them: and they were *judged every man according to their works.* (Revelation 20:12–13, emphasis added)

What is covered in this chapter is only a fraction of what we know about resurrection, and judgment. Don't limit your study to what you think you already know. Far too many missionaries teach doctrine that is not correct because they fail to pay the price to prepare. Don't fall under that condemnation.

Chapter 26

Death and the Spirit World

Understanding the part that death plays in the plan of salvation will go a long way towards reducing or eliminating the fear so many have as they approach death. Speaking of those who die while striving to live the commandments, the Lord said:

> For those that live shall inherit the earth, and those that die shall rest from all their labors, and their works shall follow them; and they shall receive a crown in the mansions of my Father, which I have prepared for them. (D&C 59:2)

From his translation of the Book of Mormon, Joseph Smith learned: "For as death hath passed upon all men, to fulfil the merciful plan of the great Creator, there must needs be a power of resurrection" (2 Nephi 9:6). How does death fulfil "the merciful plan of the great Creator"? Since all mankind entered into a fallen world (because of the Fall of Adam), we would be forever barred from returning to the presence of God. The Atonement of Christ erased that fallen condition and all mankind, righteous or evil, good or bad, will be resurrected, thus overcoming the cause of our temporal death. All people will be brought back into the presence of God to stand judgment for their works, thus overcoming the spiritual death caused by Adam's Fall which resulted in our being cut off from the presence of God.

After being returned to the presence of God for a final judgment, those who are not qualified to remain in His presence will suffer a second spiritual death. Only those who take advantage of the Atonement of Christ will be privileged to live forever in the presence of God.

Not everyone will be thrilled with the prospects of being resurrected and standing judgment for our deeds. The Lord revealed:

> Thou shalt live together in love, insomuch that thou shalt weep for the loss of them that die, and more especially for those that have not hope of a glorious resurrection.
>
> And it shall come to pass that those that die in me shall not taste of death, for it shall be sweet unto them;
>
> And they that die not in me, wo unto them, for their death is bitter. (D&C 42:45–47)

How "bitter" is the prospects of death to the wicked? Alma the Younger gives this vivid description:

> But I was racked with eternal torment, for my soul was harrowed up to the greatest degree and racked with all my sins.
>
> Yea, I did remember all my sins and iniquities, for which I was tormented with the pains of hell; yea, I saw that I had rebelled against my God, and that I had not kept his holy commandments.
>
> Yea, and I had murdered many of his children, or rather led them away unto destruction; yea, and in fine so great had been my iniquities, that the very thought of coming into the presence of my God did rack my soul with inexpressible horror.
>
> Oh, thought I, that I could be banished and become extinct both soul and body, that I might not be brought to stand in the presence of my God, to be judged of my deeds.

> And now, for three days and for three nights was I racked, even with the pains of a damned soul. (Alma 36:12–16)

The Lord revealed another fact for us to consider: "For there is a time appointed for every man, according as his works shall be" (D&C 121:25). None of us know for sure how long we are going to live. We do know that if we are diligent, we will live long enough to fulfill the assigned tasks that Heavenly Father has given us.

Joseph Smith changes our whole outlook on death when he taught: "The only difference between the old and young dying is, one lives longer in heaven and eternal light and glory than the other, and is freed a little sooner from this miserable wicked world" (*Documentary History of the Church* 4:554). That sounds very much like "the sooner the better."

One topic of great interest to both members and non-members is the post-mortal spirit world. Many books have been written about life after death. Some of the information is accurate (according to scriptures) and much that has been written doesn't appear to be correct.

As a missionary you must understand what the Lord has revealed as part of the Restoration of the gospel. Then in your teaching, stick to what has been revealed. Leave the speculation to others.

Because of the prevalence of some quotes that have been misapplied, I will include some that clarify what Joseph Smith actually said. Often people quote Joseph Smith as saying: "If you could see the glory of the telestial kingdom you would try to commit suicide to get there." While that is likely a true statement given the glory of the telestial kingdom surpasses all understanding (see D&C 76:89–90), Joseph was not referring to that kingdom. Here is what he said: "Br. Woodruff spoke. . . . He referred to a saying of Joseph Smith which he heard him utter (like this) That if the People knew what was behind the veil, they would try by every means to commit suicide that they might get there, but the Lord in his wisdom had implanted the fear of death in every person that they might cling to life and thus accomplish the designs of their creator." (Diary of Charles Lowell Walker, ed. by A. Karl Larson and Katherine M. Larson [Logan, Ut.: Utah State University Press, 1980], vol. 1, 465–66.)

Joseph Smith was referring to the spirit world (or "the next apartment"). Alma's errant son, Corianton, was concerned about life after death. Alma taught him:

> Now, concerning the state of the soul between death and the resurrection—Behold, it has been made known unto me by an angel, that the spirits of all men, as soon as they are departed from this mortal body, yea, the spirits of all men, whether they be good or evil, are taken home to that God who gave them life.
>
> And then shall it come to pass, that the spirits of those who are righteous are received into a state of happiness, which is called paradise, a state of rest, a state of peace, where they shall rest from all their troubles and from all care, and sorrow.
>
> And then shall it come to pass, that the spirits of the wicked, yea, who are evil—for behold, they have no part nor portion of the Spirit of the Lord; for behold, they chose evil works rather than good; therefore the spirit of the devil did enter into them, and take possession of their house—and these shall be cast out into outer darkness; there shall be weeping, and wailing, and gnashing of teeth, and this because of their own iniquity, being led captive by the will of the devil.
>
> Now this is the state of the souls of the wicked, yea, in darkness, and a state of awful, fearful looking for the fiery indignation of the wrath of God upon them; thus they remain in this state, as well as the righteous in paradise, until the time of their resurrection. (Alma 40:11–14)

Joseph knew from these verses about the different conditions in the spirit world. The righteous into a place called paradise—a place of peace and rest without pain, troubles, and sorrow. The wicked into a state Alma calls "outer darkness." Note that the final state of Satan and those who followed him is also known as "outer darkness." This place is also referred to as spirit prison, a portion of which is also referred to as "hell." It is a place of weeping, wailing, and gnashing of teeth. Also, a state awful and fearful looking because of the fiery indignation of the wrath of God upon them (see also Moses 7:1).

Brigham Young gave some additional insight into "hell":

> The punishment of God is God-like. It endures forever, because there never will be a time when people ought not to be damned, and there must always be a hell to send them to. How long the damned remain in hell, I know not, nor what degree of suffering they endure. If we could by any means compute how much wickedness they are guilty of, it might be possible to ascertain the amount of suffering they will receive. They will receive according as their deeds have been while in the body. God's punishment is eternal, but that does not prove that a wicked person will remain eternally in a state of punishment. (*Discourses of Brigham Young*, 383)

According to Alma's teachings:

> Therefore, according to justice, the plan of redemption could not be brought about, only on conditions of repentance of men in this probationary state, yea, this preparatory state; for except it were for these conditions, mercy could not take effect except it should destroy the work of justice. Now the work of justice could not be destroyed; if so, God would cease to be God. (Alma 42:13)

It is important to understand that "this life is the time for men to prepare to meet God; yea, behold the day of this life is the day for men to perform their labors" (Alma 34:32). However, in order for repentance, payment, and improvement to take place in the spirit world, we must understand how the term "this life" is used.

Alma gives this definition:

> And we see that death comes upon mankind, yea, the death which has been spoken of by Amulek, which is the temporal death; nevertheless there was a space granted unto man in which he might repent; therefore *this life*

> became a probationary state; a time to prepare to meet God; *a time to prepare* for that endless state which has been spoken of by us, *which is after the resurrection of the dead.* (Alma 12:24, emphasis added)

According to that scripture, the time period covered by the term "this life" begins with our mortal birth, continues through mortality, and extends into the spirit world up to the time of the Resurrection.

In order for God to obey the laws of justice, which He instituted, man had to repent during the probationary space. As well as any place, this demonstrates the loving kindness of God. He gives to every spirit son or daughter a lifetime to repent and get it right. If that doesn't satisfy their needs, He extends that probationary time all the way to the time of the Resurrection.

For your investigators:

Without a clear understanding of the ultimate goal of God—to bring to pass the immortality and eternal life of man (Moses 1:39), God takes on a very threatening appearance. The Lord revealed in the account of Lazarus and the rich man (Luke 16:22–23) that a gulf existed between the righteous and those in torment in hell. Until the death of Christ, that gulf continued to prevent the righteous from going to visit and stopped the wicked from going to where the righteous dwell.

In Joseph F. Smith's vision of the spirit world, he saw how that gulf was bridged by the Savior's instructions while He was in the spirit world while His body was in the tomb.

> But his ministry among those who were dead was limited to the brief time intervening between the crucifixion and his resurrection;
>
> And I wondered at the words of Peter—wherein he said that the Son of God preached unto the spirits in prison, who sometime were disobedient, when once the long-suffering of God waited in the days of Noah—and how it was possible for him to preach to those spirits and perform the necessary labor among them in so short a time.

> And as I wondered, my eyes were opened, and my understanding quickened, and I perceived that the Lord went not in person among the wicked and the disobedient who had rejected the truth, to teach them;
>
> But behold, from among the righteous, he organized his forces and appointed messengers, clothed with power and authority, and commissioned them to go forth and carry the light of the gospel to them that were in darkness, even to all the spirits of men; and thus was the gospel preached to the dead.
>
> And the chosen messengers went forth to declare the acceptable day of the Lord and proclaim liberty to the captives who were bound, even unto all who would repent of their sins and receive the gospel. (D&C 138:27–31)

Obviously, there is much more that we don't understand about the structure and limitations of the spirit prison. However, Joseph Smith made a statement indicating that "hell" might be but a part of the spirit prison. He said:

> I do not believe the Methodist doctrine of sending honest men and noble-minded men to *hell*, along with the murderer and the adulterer. They may hurl all their hell and fiery billows upon me, for they will roll off me as fast as they come on. But I have an order of things to save the poor fellows at any rate, and get them saved; for I will send men to preach to them *in prison* and save them if I can. (*Teachings of the Prophet Joseph Smith*, 366, emphasis added)

It seems that the "hell" portion of the spirit prison is designated as a place of suffering and payment for sins not repented of while the rest of the spirit prison is for good and honorable men who had not received the gospel. They were there to be taught by the designated missionaries from the spirit paradise. Presumably, according to a quote by Elder James E. Talmage used earlier in the chapter on "Repent or Suffer," once the unrepentant had paid for their sins, the prison doors would open and they would be welcomed into a place where they could be taught the gospel—not paradise, because they had not accepted the gospel and been baptized.

From all accounts it sounds like the paradise is the holding place for those individuals who are candidates for the celestial kingdom. Spirits in paradise are not subject to the continual temptations of Satan. They rest from all their labors and continue learning necessary principles to enable them to enter the celestial kingdom.

Once again, do not teach beyond what has been revealed. As you continue to study the scriptures and the latter-day prophets, you will gain greater insights that will enable you to answer even more questions concerning the post-mortal spirit world.

Chapter 27

Three Degrees of Glory and Exaltation

Not everyone living on earth will qualify for exaltation in God's celestial kingdom. Therefore, a wise and loving Father has provided a place where each son and daughter will be comfortable and enjoy.

One of the most mind-expanding visions ever given is recorded in Doctrine and Covenants section 76. Although there are six visions described, we will only consider those dealing with the kingdoms or eventual habitations of man.

The Lord starts with visions of contrast. First, He describes where the sons of perdition go (verses 30–49). The Lord had just finished describing the fall of Satan, and his relentless making "war with the Saints of God" (see verse 29). As you carefully read these verses, be aware that those who go to outer darkness forever were members of the Church who gave into the temptations of Satan. Note how in verse 31 the Lord explains that the sons of perdition "have suffered themselves to be overcome." Rather than just leaving the Church, these formerly valiant Saints, after they fall away, openly deny and defy the truth. In the next verse, the Lord says it would have been better for them if they had never been born.

In addition to being denied access to the forgiving grace of the Atonement of Christ, they suffer for their own sins, they deny the

Holy Ghost (something non-members never had), they put God and Christ to an open shame, and their doom is to suffer with the devil and his angels in everlasting and eternal punishment (see verse 44) .We must leave to God what is their final destiny since the Lord said: "And the end thereof, neither the place thereof, nor their torment, no man knows; Neither was it revealed, neither is, neither will be revealed unto man, except to them who are made partakers thereof" (verses 45–46).

Hopefully, there will be very few who receive that terrible judgment. However, Joseph Smith said after describing what a man must do to commit the unpardonable sin: "This is the case with many apostates of the Church of Jesus Christ of Latter-day Saints" (*History of the Church,* 6:314).

Next, the Lord contrasts the sons of perdition with those who inherit the celestial kingdom (see verse 50–70). Many of the principles we have discussed previously in other chapters are also found in the Lord's description of those who go to the celestial kingdom. We will only summarize them as a review and to show how all of those principles fit into the eternal destiny of those who enter the celestial kingdom.

As mentioned in the chapter "Resurrection and Judgment," these celestial people will come forth in the morning of the First Resurrection. If they have passed away prior to the Second Coming, they will be resurrected and come with Christ as He returns to usher in the Millennium (see D&C 88:97–98; see also D&C 76:63–65).

None of the prerequisites for celestial living are beyond our abilities to live. They have received the testimony of Jesus, have been baptized, they have received the Holy Ghost, and they strive to keep the commandments. They have repented and been forgiven of their sins (sounds like Article of Faith #4, doesn't it!).

They have overcome every temptation of the devil by their faith in Christ (see Alma 37:33). They have proven themselves worthy to the point of being "sealed by the Holy Spirit of promise" (see chapter "Marriage and Children").

They are invited in as full members of the "Church of the Firstborn"—the name of the Church in the celestial kingdom (see verse 94). They are given all power as the Father promised in Doctrine and Covenants 84:38. They are crowned as kings and queens, and are priests after the order of The Only Begotten Son. They are awarded the title and powers of gods. They have power over all things, including life and death.

Most interesting in verse 60, the Lord says: "And they shall overcome all things." "Shall" denotes a condition that does not presently exist but will sometime in the future. It appears that our quest to overcome everything and become totally perfect will continue long after we arrive in the celestial kingdom. So, don't despair because you are not yet perfect.

The promise is that celestial kingdom people "dwell in the presence of God and his Christ forever and ever" (verse 62).

A careful reading of verses 50–70 (and re-reading many times) will enlarge your understanding and should create a desire within you to pay whatever price is necessary to qualify for the celestial kingdom.

Now the Lord describes those who go to the terrestrial kingdom. In verses 71–80, the Lord described attributes of terrestrial beings. Be careful not to try to apply these conditions to people you know on earth since "it ain't over 'til it's over!" and repentance continues into the spirit world.

Here is the Lord's listing of those who will inherit that kingdom: they die "without law"—meaning outside the law. The Lord uses "within" to refer to people in the Church and "without" meaning outside the Church. When the Lord cleansed the earth by flood in Noah's day, the people who were drowned were kept in spirit prison (see the chapter "Spirit World"). It appears that the sum total of their judgment will only result in their receiving the terrestrial kingdom.

Verses 74–75 may lead to a misunderstanding if not taken together with verse 79. The Lord says these people didn't receive the testimony of Jesus in the flesh but received it in the spirit world. First, realize they must have had the chance to receive it in mortality but didn't take advantage of their opportunity. Additionally, they were honorable men who were blinded by people who dissuaded them from joining the Church.

One might question why we do temple work for people who had a chance and didn't accept it if the highest kingdom they can achieve is the terrestrial kingdom and no ordinances are mentioned as prerequisite for the terrestrial kingdom. The answer comes in considering verse 79 along with verses 74 and 75. These people who didn't join the Church here on earth because they *were* deceived, later received it in the spirit world but who still "*are not valiant*" in their testimony of Jesus will receive the terrestrial kingdom. What if they who "*were*" blinded in mortality so they didn't join the Church accepted the Church when taught in the spirit world, and "*are now valiant*"? The answer is—they will receive the celestial kingdom.

Although the glory of the terrestrial kingdom is less than the celestial kingdom as the light of the moon is from the sun, it is still more glorious than we can currently comprehend. One other major difference between these people and those in the celestial kingdom: "These are they who receive of the presence of the Son, but not of the fulness of the Father" (verse 77).

Finally, the Lord reveals the attitudes and behaviors of those who will eventually go to the telestial kingdom. The telestial kingdom qualifications and conditions are found in verses 81–90, 98–106, and 109–112. Here is a summary of what the Lord revealed about the telestial people: They didn't receive (either here or in the spirit world) either the testimony of Jesus or the gospel. They don't deny the Holy Ghost (which would make them sons of perdition) because they never had the Holy Ghost. They spend time in the "hell" portion of the spirit world paying for their own sins. They will not be resurrected until the end of the Millennium. These are "liars, and sorcerers, and adulterers, and whoremongers, and whosoever loves and makes a lie" (verse 103). This suggests that they never repent and receive forgiveness because they won't accept Christ and His Atonement. They suffer the wrath of God on earth and also in the spirit world.

This sounds pretty bad, but the Lord revealed: "And thus we saw, in the heavenly vision, the glory of the telestial, which surpasses all understanding; And no man knows it except him to whom God has revealed it" (verses 89–90).

These people cannot go where God and Christ dwell in "worlds without end" (see verse 112) but will be ministered to by the Holy Ghost and angels who are appointed to minister to them from the terrestrial kingdom (see verses 86–88).

Exaltation—living in the presence of God, enjoying "all that the Father hath," doing what the Father does, and having been given the gift of eternal life. This is the ultimate goal of mankind and the reason for our coming to earth. However, this is not something that should be taught to investigators until they have a firm foundation based on faith in the Lord, Jesus Christ, have repented of their sins, have agreed to or entered into the covenant of baptism, and received the Holy Ghost. Without the enlightening power of the Holy Ghost, it would be impossible for them to understand these lofty concepts.

Far too many missionaries want to jump to the end point—the godship of man—before their investigators are prepared to receive and understand the doctrine. Therefore, this portion of the chapter is for the benefit of you—the future missionary.

Exaltation is the description of those who inherit the highest degree of the celestial kingdom. As baptism is the gate to the celestial kingdom (see John 3:3–5), eternal marriage is the gate to the highest degree in that kingdom (see D&C 131:1–4).

As we have noted throughout this book, Satan is doing and will continue to do all he can to prevent people from joining the Church, thus eliminating (or at least postponing) their ability to return to the presence of God. Likewise, Satan's relentless efforts to prevent faithful spirit children of God from gaining exaltation should put us on notice of his tactics.

If you consider what God does (and what exalted men and women will eventually do), you can identify the areas where Satan will focus his destructive efforts. For our purpose here, we will only discuss two exalted powers. First, we know that we are offspring of our Heavenly Parents. In Doctrine and Covenants 131:1–4, Joseph Smith instructs us as to what is required to have the power to have eternal increase.

> In the celestial glory there are three heavens or degrees;
>
> And in order to obtain the highest, a man must enter into this order of the priesthood [meaning the new and everlasting covenant of marriage];
>
> And if he does not, he cannot obtain it.
>
> He may enter into the other, but that is the end of his kingdom; he cannot have an increase.

Since marriage was defined by God from the very beginning of time and has been declared in "The Family—A Proclamation to the World" by modern prophets, and since Satan is called "the enemy to all righteousness" (see Mosiah 4:14), it should come as no surprise that he will do all in his evil power to prevent men and women from marrying in the temple. If they do marry in the temple, he will constantly attack them, tempting them to disregard the covenants they made in the temple.

If you review the questions asked by the bishop and stake president in a temple recommend interview, you will see what one must do to qualify to enter the temple and receive those ordinances necessary for exaltation. One of the major disqualifiers is immorality.

Why is chastity so important? Because controlling the very power which enables men and women to become parents here on earth, is the test to see whether those powers will be restored to men and women when they are resurrected. Let's review what you learned in the chapter "Marriage and Children."

> Therefore, if a man marry him a wife in the world, and he marry her not by me nor by my word, and he covenant with her so long as he is in the world and she with him, their covenant and marriage are not of force when they are dead, and when they are out of the world; therefore, they are not bound by any law when they are out of the world.
>
> Therefore, when they are out of the world they neither marry nor are given in marriage; but are appointed angels in heaven, which angels are ministering servants, to minister for those who are worthy of a far more, and an exceeding, and an eternal weight of glory.
>
> For these angels did not abide my law; therefore, they cannot be enlarged, but remain separately and singly, without exaltation, in their saved condition, to all eternity; and from henceforth are not gods, but are angels of God forever and ever. (D&C 132:15–17)

If Satan can tempt men and women (young or old) to violate the laws of chastity, he is moving them closer to disqualifying themselves from the blessing of exaltation. This is like the final test before receiving a commercial pilot's license. If you fail that test, no one would question why you would be denied the license—thousands of people's lives would eventually depend on you being qualified and able to safely control the airplane. If you fail to pass the test of controlling your procreative powers, it would not be seen as discriminatory or unfair if those powers were not given to you eternally.

Second, God is a creator of worlds without number. Although there is much we do not understand, we know it is by His almighty power (i.e. Priesthood) that worlds are created. If a man does not learn to use that priesthood power according to God's will while in this life, how dangerous would it be to give him unlimited power in the next life? Perhaps that is one reason that misusing and turning away from the priesthood puts the man in the unenviable position the Lord described in Doctrine and Covenants 84:41: "But whoso breaketh this covenant after he hath received it, and altogether turneth therefrom, shall not have forgiveness of sins in this world nor in the world to come."

Exaltation will only be a blessing to those who learn to think, talk, act, and become like God. To be given His unlimited power without having developed His perfect attributes and characteristics would be devastating to the perfect environment we know as heaven.

For your investigators:

The doctrine of the three degrees of glory will be such new and exciting doctrine to those who are prepared to receive the gospel that they will question why they have never heard of such a thing. Gently explain that it is taught in the Bible but without the light of the restored gospel, their ministers are not able to teach them what they, themselves, do not understand.

The Lord taught His disciples just before leaving them: "In my Father's house are many mansions: if it were not so, I would have told you. I go to prepare a place for you" (John 14:2).

Paul boldly taught:

> There are also celestial bodies, and bodies terrestrial: but the glory of the celestial is one, and the glory of the terrestrial is another.
>
> There is one glory of the sun, and another glory of the moon, and another glory of the stars: for one star differeth from another star in glory.
>
> So also is the resurrection of the dead. (1 Corinthians 15:40–42)

What you take for granted because you have been taught the three degrees of glory all of your life, will be new and strange doctrine to many Christians who have never been introduced to such doctrine. Take it slow and listen carefully to the promptings of the Spirit telling you when you have taught all they are currently ready to receive. If you fail to stop at that point, you can almost bet they will not be actively investigating the gospel in the future.

Many Christians reel at the idea of men and women become like God. Yet the Savior teaches the doctrine in unmistakable language:

> I and my Father are one.
>
> Then the Jews took up stones again to stone him.
>
> Jesus answered them, Many good works have I shewed you from my Father; for which of those works do ye stone me?
>
> The Jews answered him, saying, For a good work we stone thee not; but for blasphemy; and because that thou, being a man, makest thyself God.
>
> Jesus answered them, Is it not written in your law, I said, *Ye are gods*?
>
> If he called them gods, unto whom the word of God came, and the scripture cannot be broken;

> Say ye of him, whom the Father hath sanctified, and sent into the world, Thou blasphemest; because I said, I am the Son of God? (John 10:30–36, emphasis added)

Although almost everyone admits that when our children grow up, marry, and have children, it only adds to our status, they vehemently oppose the idea that men and women growing up to become like their Eternal Parents only adds to the glory of God.

Perhaps that is a good reason for you to hold back talking about exaltation (although it is the very heart of the purpose for mortality) until your investigators have become members and their testimonies are rock solid.

Epilogue

Your Time—Prepare Now!

Unparalleled, this is the most wonderful time to be on earth. With all of the modern conveniences, technological advances, supersonic modes of transportation, instantaneous means of communication—the list is nearly endless. No generation before us has had it so good.

This is also the most dangerous and demanding time to live on earth. Natural calamities claim the lives of hundreds of thousands, diseases strike both the old and the young, God-revealed standards are ignored or attempted to be reversed by legislation, drugs, alcohol, pornography and a list of evils are drowning us as a civilization, marriages and families are being destroyed, terrorists are robbing us of our sense of security. These are difficult times.

Your time on earth is to you as Mordecai explained to Queen Esther when only she could save the Jews from total destruction: "who knoweth whether thou art come to the kingdom for such a time as this?" (Esther 4:14)

Your time on earth was determined before the world was created. President Ezra Taft Benson said of your generation:

> For nearly six thousand years, God has held you in reserve to make your appearance in the final days before the Second Coming of the Lord. . . . While our generation will be comparable in wickedness to the days of Noah,

> when the Lord cleansed the earth by flood, there is a major difference this time. It is that God has saved for the final inning some of his strongest children, who will help bear off the Kingdom triumphantly. And that is where you come in, for you are the generation that must be prepared to meet your God.
>
> All through the ages the prophets have looked down through the corridors of time to our day. Billions of the deceased and those yet to be born have their eyes on us. Make no mistake about it—you are a marked generation. There has never been more expected of the faithful in such a short period of time as there is of us. Never before on the face of this earth have the forces of evil and the forces of good been as well organized. Now is the great day of the devil's power, with the greatest mass murderers of all time living among us. But now is also the great day of the Lord's power, with the greatest number ever of priesthood holders on the earth. And the showdown is fast approaching. ("In His Steps," [Brigham Young University devotional, March 4, 1979], speeches.byu.edu)

More recently, Sister Elaine S. Dalton of the Young Women General Presidency said,

> President Gordon B. Hinckley has said of you: "You are . . . the finest [and strongest] generation of young people ever in the history of this Church." I believe that you have been prepared and reserved to be on the earth at this time when the challenges and opportunities are the greatest. I believe that the Lord is counting on you to be a leader for righteousness and to stand as a witness "at all times and in all things, and in all places." Indeed, it can be said of you that you are the "bright shining hope" of the future. ("It Shows in Your Face," *Ensign*, May 2007).

Joseph Smith said: "Every man who has a calling to minister to the inhabitants of the world was ordained to that very purpose in the Grand Council of heaven before this world was. I suppose I was ordained to this very office in that Grand Council" (*Teachings of the Prophet Joseph Smith*, 365).

Think of it—you have been waiting for over 6,000 years for this very moment. Is it any wonder that the Lord said: "Lift up your heart and rejoice, for the hour of your mission is come; and your tongue shall be loosed, and you shall declare glad tidings of great joy unto this generation" (D&C 31:3)?

This mission you are preparing for isn't something you "have to do"—it is something you "get to do." You were called, prepared, foreordained, and honored to serve a mission! Compared to the number of people who have ever lived on earth, you are one in millions so honored to serve on the Lord's first team in the closing seconds of the fourth quarter of the super bowl of all time.

Is it a scary world you are going to serve in? Undoubtedly! There will be dangers all around you. However, remember the purpose the Lord has chosen you to preach His gospel:

> Wherefore, I call upon the weak things of the world, those who are unlearned and despised, to thresh the nations by the power of my Spirit;
>
> And their arm shall be my arm, and I will be their shield and their buckler; and I will gird up their loins, and they shall fight manfully for me; and their enemies shall be under their feet; and *I will let fall the sword in their behalf, and by the fire of mine indignation will I preserve them*" (D&C 35:13–14, emphasis added).

With that kind of protection, you have nothing to fear as long as you follow the rules your mission president has established. Repeating a scripture used before, the Lord said:

> And whoso receiveth you, there I will be also, for I will go before your face. I will be on your right hand and on your left, and my Spirit shall be in your hearts, and mine angels round about you, to bear you up. (D&C 84:88)

Given the rise in terrorist attacks, some prospective missionaries may be fearful of going on a mission. Statistically you have a far greater chance of being hurt or killed if you stay home than if you serve a mission. Elder M. Russell Ballard stated: "The safest place in the world for 19- to 21-year-old young men and 21-year-old young women is in the service of the Lord in the mission field, scattered out over the four corners of the earth" ("'This Work Will Continue to Go Forward': Elder Ballard Discusses Missionary Safety," *Ensign*, April 2006).

There is a major difference between you being killed in a car accident, snowboarding, swimming, rock climbing, paragliding, or in some other "fun and games" activity and you being killed while serving a mission. If you die just having fun—you are dead! On the other hand, if you die while serving a mission, the Lord said: "And whoso layeth down his life in my cause, for my name's sake, shall find it again, even *life eternal*" (D&C 98:13, emphasis added). Given that promise and the statistical safety you enjoy as a missionary over those who do not serve, it seems pretty obvious that the Lord wants you to fulfil your foreordained mission.

You needn't be alarmed that you might die before your time. The Lord revealed: "For there is a time appointed for every man, according as his works shall be" (D&C 121:25).

The Church leaders are very aware and very concerned about your safety. They take extra precautions when dangerous situations arise. They have evacuation plans in place to move you to a safe area if you are in danger. All that being said, your mission will be the greatest life-changer possible, if you continue to use the lessons you learned while serving.

A mission will chart the direction for the rest of your life. It will influence who you marry, where you marry, how you treat your spouse and children, what recreational activities you engage in, the amount of service you give, your enjoyment of life in general, and your hope for eternal life in the world to come.

Nothing you can do—no matter what it is—can come close to matching the benefits you receive for serving a successful mission. You cannot be "over prepared" to serve. Start now. Increase your intensity. Increase your focus. Prepare for your mission.

About the Author

Randy L. Bott

Brother Bott is married to the love of his life, Vickie (fifty years and counting). Together they have six children, sixteen grandchildren, and one great-granddaughter.

Brother Bott has a bachelor's and master's degree from Utah State University (a bachelor's in psychology, and a master's in secondary education) and a doctor's degree in educational leadership from BYU. He has served as a bishop, in two stake presidencies, and as a mission president. He served his first mission in Samoa.

After Brother Bott retired from BYU in 2012, he and his wife served missions at BYU–Hawaii and Sydney, Australia. They are currently preparing for another mission.

Brother Bott taught twenty years with CES in Utah and North Carolina. He taught nineteen years at BYU–Provo. He has authored many books and articles. His passion is teaching and counseling. He loves people and loves problem solving and creating new programs to help people succeed.